Melted

My snowman sees me
From inside his glass dome,
While I peek at him,
Inside his wee home.

He's cubby and chunky,
A jolly snow-elf,
As I smile at hime
He grins from his shelf.

His nose is a cherry,
His head has a hat
And his belly boasts buttons,
All lumpy and black.

His plump, snowy arm
Is waving at me,
And when I shake, shake him,
A snowstorm I see.

My snowman and I
Were friends form the start,
For this little snowman
Has melted my heart.

by Jeanene Engelhardt

Holidays

& Seasonal Celebrations

Holidays & Seasonal Celebrations is published four times a year (March, July, October, December) by the Teaching & Learning Company, 1204 Buchanan Street, Carthage, IL 62321-0010. Subscription costs are $17.95 for 1 year, $31.95 for 2 years and $47.95 for 3 years. Single issue cost is $4.95.

Application to Mail at Second-Class Postage Rates is Pending at Carthage, Illinois. Postmaster: Send address changes to *Holidays & Seasonal Celebrations*, P.O. Box 10, Carthage, IL 62321-0010.

Editorial Comments & Submissions should be sent to Magazine Editor, Teaching & Learning Company, P.O. Box 10, Carthage, IL 62321. No manuscripts will be returned unless sent with an appropriately stamped envelope.

Holidays
& Seasonal Celebrations

Jan./Feb./Mar. 1997
Volume 2, Number 4, Issue 8

Created with ♥ *by*

Editor
Donna Borst

Production
Kim Rankin

Art Director
Teresa Mathis

Managing Editor
Jill Eckhardt

Contributing Artists
Janet Armbrust
Gayle Vella
Becky J. Radtke
Cara H. Bradshaw
Gary Hoover
Luda Stekol
Chris Nye

Cover Photo
Images & More

Cover Models
Carissa Rabe

Cover Craft
Judy Hierstein

Director of Operations
Chris Goetz

Marketing Director
Tami Long

Director of Special Projects
Rauna Twaddle

Publisher
Don and Judy Mitchell

Teaching & Learning Company

Teaching & Learning Company
1204 Buchanan St.
P.O. Box 10
Carthage, IL 62321
e-mail: tandlcom@adams.net
1-217-357-2591
Fax: 1-217-357-6789

For a Friend!

Write or call for a free issue of Holidays & Seasonal Celebrations. We'll send your friend a free sample copy!

We Want to Hear from You!

We're looking for ideas, units, reproducibles and classroom-tested activities to include in future issues of *Holidays & Seasonal Celebrations*. All materials must either be seasonally related or pertain to a holiday of some sort. Manuscripts should be suitable for preK-grade 3 and accompanied by a self-addressed, appropriately stamped envelope. Please direct all submissions to Holidays & Seasonal Celebrations.

Illustrators Wanted

The Teaching & Learning Company is looking for artists to illustrate educational activity books and pages for *Holidays & Seasonal Celebrations*. If you feel your work might be suitable for us, please send nonreturnable samples to Teresa Mathis. Line illustrations (b&w or color) of multiethnic children (preK-6) are a must in order to be considered.

Calling All Writers!

The Teaching & Learning Company is looking for manuscripts for the preK-6 market. If you have a book you'd like to share with us, send us a copy and a self-addressed, appropriately stamped envelope. Send your manuscript ideas to Jill Eckhardt.

Holiday Hints for Home & School

This feature of *Holidays & Seasonal Celebrations* will offer a wide variety of holiday-related teacher helpers. If you have any quick, original holiday or seasonal ideas that you feel will benefit your fellow teachers, please send them to Holiday Hints. If your idea is published, we will send you a $15.00 gift certificate for Teaching & Learning Company products.

Celebrate Children!

Do you have a photo of a classroom holiday celebration you'd like to share? Have any of your students ever written a special holiday poem or drawn a seasonal masterpiece? We would like to celebrate children by publishing some of their extra-special efforts. Please send to Celebrate Children, and include your name, child's name, school, grade level, address and daytime phone. Sorry, photos cannot be returned.

To subscribe

to Holidays & Seasonal Celebrations, write to us or call toll free 1-800-852-1234.

Meltdown

I'm worried about Sammy.
He has lost a lot of weight.
His scarf is hanging off him
and he does not look so great.
Just yesterday he stood tall,
his barrel chest puffing out,
as healthy as a grizzly
(but perhaps a little stout).
Although I hate to say it,
there's a dent in Sammy's head.
His hat is sliding forward.
Sam's eyes are becoming spread.
He's standing in a puddle.
I'm afraid that he may drown.
The sun keeps beating on him.
He will soon be falling down.
I have to leave the window.
I can't watch poor Sammy wilt.
He was the greatest snowman
that anyone ever built!

by Timothy Tocher

Holidays & Seasonal Celebrations, Issue 8, Teaching & Learning Co. © 1997, Carthage, IL 62321

Snowclothes

Today I put my snowclothes on,
But nothing came out right.
The snow pants wound up backwards.
My scarf was much too tight.

The mittens went on crooked.
The jacket wouldn't zip.
My bootlace got all knotted
And my hat began to slip.

But now my clothes are on just right.
I fixed them all quite fast.
I'm warm and ready. Out I go—
In the snow, at last!

by Mary Ryer

Holidays & Seasonal Celebrations, Issue 8, Teaching & Learning Co. © 1997, Carthage, IL 62321

Weather WISE

Weather is a constant source of intelligent questions from curious kids. The ever-changing weather of late winter/early spring provides the setting for scientific exploration of many things. Try these Weather WISE activities to help kids learn about the weather and its effects on their natural environment. Simple procedures and the use of everyday materials make the Weather WISE activities simple and easy for children and educators.

Encourage young learners to formulate questions, investigate their environment, make discoveries and become weather wise!

by Robynne Eagan

Report the Weather

There's no better time than late winter/early spring to keep track of the weather. It's exciting, ever-changing and fascinating to talk about.

As part of a language arts program, ask students to research and give the weather reports. It is an important task that can be presented on a daily basis along with the calendar. Have students observe, study and research the weather to help them prepare a statement to communicate particular conditions at a particular place and time. Young children can merely look out the window and report what they see. Students in grades one or above are capable of studying the classroom weather station (if you have one), checking the newspaper, or listening to the news to help them prepare their weather reports. Encourage students to use weather maps, technical information, props and creativity in these reports.

Weather Walk

(Discussion questions can be adapted to suit any grade level.)
What better way to understand the weather than to take a walk in it. Take walks on days which offer varying weather conditions.

Encourage students to observe and discuss the weather they experience.
- How does the sky look? What types of clouds can be seen?
- Is there any precipitation? What kind? How much?
- How does the air feel? Is it damp or dry?
- Does it feel cold or warm? What is the temperature?
- Is there wind? Which direction is it blowing?
- Is there evidence of any animals? How will this weather affect them? How will this weather affect people you know?
- What people are most affected by the changing late winter/early spring weather? What effects will the weather have on farms, gardens, waterways, roads, travel and special events?

Rainbows

Early spring is a perfect time to take a look at one of the wonders of nature—the rainbow. Seize the moment when there's a rainbow in the sky to present your lesson on rainbows!

Rainbow Recipe

Do you know what is needed to make a rainbow? Sometimes the weather conditions have just the right ingredients to make a rainbow: sunlight and droplets of water. When do these conditions generally occur? Ask students to keep a Rainbow Record—to record the weather conditions when rainbows were sighted. Discuss their findings.

Make Your Own Rainbow

How can you make your own rainbow? Talk about the ingredients that are needed—sunlight and water. On a sunny day, you can add your own water droplets to the air by using a hose with a spray nozzle set for the finest spray. Spray in a direction away from the sun and have children stand by you. If children stand in just the right place, they will be able to see the tiny rainbow. Rainbow gazers may need to move up and down or to the side to catch sight of the rainbow. Allow each child to make a rainbow.

What Causes the Rainbow?

Sunlight, or white light, is really a mixture of many colors. When the sunlight shines through a concentration of water droplets at just the right angle, the ray of light is bent and breaks into the colors we see in the rainbow.

R - O - Y - G - B - I - V

What on Earth can these letters stand for? Roy-g-biv is one way of saying it. These letters represent something to do with the rainbow. Can your children figure out the mystery? Red - Orange - Yellow - Green - Blue - Indigo - Violet, of course. The colors of the rainbow always appear in this order. Have your students make up memory aids to help them remember this sequence.

Paint a Rainbow

Use poster paints and large paintbrushes to paint a rainbow with the right colors in the right order.

• Indigo is a dark violet-blue color.

Have You Ever Seen a . . .

Double rainbow?
Moonbow?
Sun dog?
Pot of gold at the end of the rainbow?

Finish the Sentence

At the end of the rainbow there is . . .

6

Winter's Over: A Spring Tally

In the Northern Hemisphere, spring officially begins on or around March 20th or 21st when the spring equinox occurs. On this date, day and night are of equal length everywhere in the world. The Earth is at a point in its revolution around the sun when the sun seems to cross the equator.

Spring may officially begin on this date, but in many places it doesn't feel like it. Discuss the quarterly official changes of season and the arrival of seasonal weather. When does spring really arrive in your Kid Space? Venture into the great outdoors to look for signs of the arrival of spring weather.

Complete the spring tally sheet below to determine when spring weather has arrived.

_____ The temperature gets warmer.

_____ The days get longer.

_____ The nights grow shorter.

_____ People wear less clothing.

_____ The snow melts.

_____ The landscape, lawns and school yard turn green.

_____ The shoots of flowers and bulbs peek through the earth.

_____ Buds appear on the trees.

_____ Birds return.

_____ People prepare to celebrate Valentine's Day, St. Patrick's Day, Passover, Groundhog Day, April Fools' Day and Easter.

_____ Children play more outdoor games and sports.

Holidays & Seasonal Celebrations, Issue 8, Teaching & Learning Co. © 1997, Carthage, IL 62321

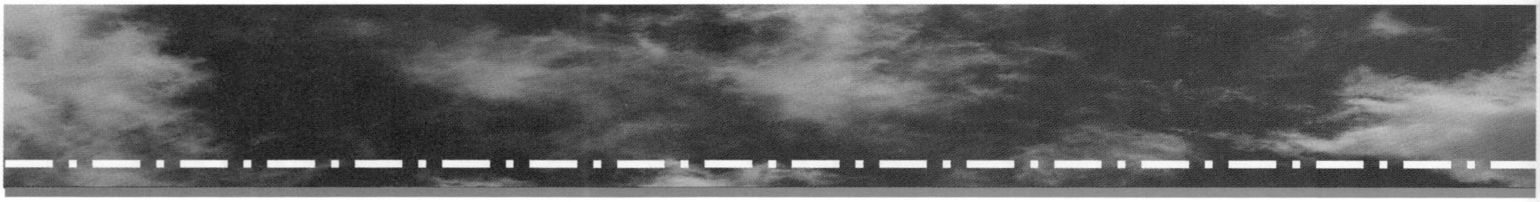

The Snow and Rain Quiz

1. Precipitation is the stuff that falls from the clouds onto our heads. Circle the things that fall from the clouds.

   rain   leaf   hail   snow   dogs   sleet

2. Choose words from the word box to fill in the blanks below.

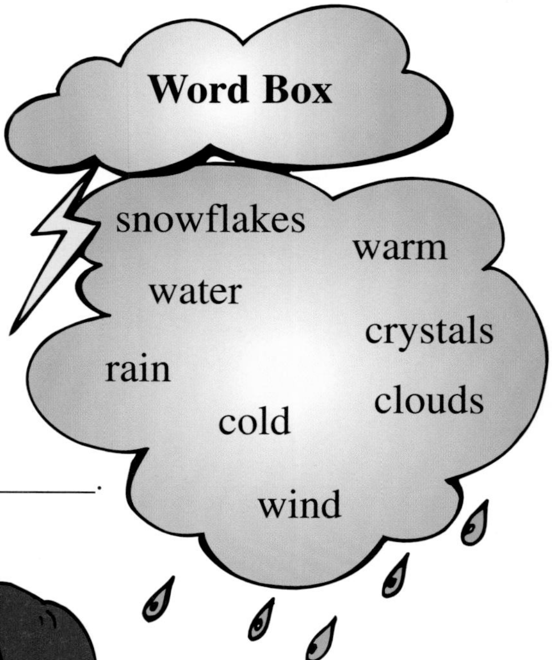

   a. High up in the sky it is cold, and water vapor that is in the air condenses and forms tiny droplets of _____.

   b. Water droplets gather together in the sky to form _____.

   c. When the water droplets get too heavy, they fall as _____.

   d. When the weather is _____, the droplets fall as rain.

   e. When it is cold enough, tiny droplets will freeze to form ice _____.

   f. Ice crystals gather together to form _____.

Word Box

snowflakes

warm

water

rain

crystals

cold

clouds

wind

8

Have an Earth-Friendly Winter

Although the official Earth Day isn't until April 22, children should practice being "Earth friendly" every day of the year. Here are some special winter practices.

Indoors

 Save fuel; instead of turning up the thermostat, put on an extra sweater or sweatshirt.

 Save electricity; turn off TV when not watching, lights when you leave the room.

 Open drapes or blinds during the daytime to let sunlight bring added warmth to rooms.

 Cover windows with shades or drapes at night to keep the daytime heat in and the nighttime cold out.

 Use rugs or rolled newspapers to keep cold drafts from coming in under door spaces.

Outdoors

 Remember that animals are part of Earth's treasures. Shovel paths for pets that go out.

 Be sure not to leave pets outdoors for long on very cold days.

 Fill bird feeders or hang up pinecones coated with peanut butter and rolled in birdseed.

 On icy steps and walks, use kitty litter or sand instead of harmful salt products.

These Three Months Are Full of Holidays with Parties, Gifts and Cards

 Remove gift wrap carefully so it can be reused.

 Wrap your own gifts with newspaper, comic pages or decorated grocery bags.

 If valentines or other cards are to be passed out in school, make "cookie cards" instead. (Be sure to find out if any classmate cannot have sweets before doing this.)

 Use soft washcloths, napkins or shredded tissue instead of plastic "grass" inside baskets.

 Find ways to reuse greeting cards (as gift tags, bookmarks, puzzles, mobiles, magnets).

by Elaine Hansen Cleary

Activities to Use with Earth-Friendly Winter Lessons

Fun Ways to Reuse Greeting Cards

 Cut out circles or squares to use as gift tags.

 Cut strips to use as bookmarks. (Your school librarian will welcome these bookmarks.)

 Make a jigsaw puzzle by cutting the front picture into interlocking parts.

 Make a mobile by cutting out pictures of animals or flowers. Then string them at different lengths to a wire coat hanger or piece of doweling.

 Cut and glue a cute picture to a magnetic strip to make a refrigerator magnet.

 Cut off the inside of a French-fold card, using the outside half to make a new card or note paper. Make up a poem or write your own greeting inside.

 Cut large letters apart and see how many other words you can make.

 Glue pictures cut from several cards to a piece of plain paper to make a new picture. You may want to color in the background with crayons or markers.

 Make a picture for your wall by creating a paper frame for the front of a pretty card.

 Build a house of cards by stacking them against and on top of each other.

* Safety Note: When using scissors, have an adult or older child supervise or help!

Holidays & Seasonal Celebrations, Issue 8, Teaching & Learning Co. © 1997, Carthage, IL 62321

Earth-Friendly Practices

Grades PreK–1

 Give each child a construction paper circle with a smiling face on one side and a frowning face on the other. (Or have children practice smiling and frowning—this saves paper!) Then read each of the practices listed, rewording some to give them a negative slant. Children evaluate the practice by showing the appropriate facial expression.

 Teacher (or child) names a winter Earth-friendly practice. Have children respond with a designated action according to whether it's an indoor or outdoor activity.

 Teacher names a situation or shows a picture (eg., icy sidewalk). Have children give an Earth-friendly practice to go with it.

 Make a big collage of illustrations, some showing good practices, others showing harmful ones. Let children put green circles around good practices and black Xs over bad ones.

Grades 2-3

 Write a list of 15 statements (some Earth-friendly DOs, others harmful DON'Ts). In front of each statement, write two letters, making certain the correct answers under DO or DON'T spell out ALWAYS HELP (or LOVE) EARTH. As children read the list, have them circle the correct letter for each statement. Then write the letters in order below. If correct, they will spell out Always help (or love) Earth.

 Make posters to put in classrooms and hallways, as well as at home, showing or listing Earth-friendly winter practices.

 Give each student two 3" x 5" index cards. On one, have them write a bad situation (eg., "The sidewalk is icy."), and on the other a good solution (eg., "Sprinkle kitty litter on it."). Mix up the cards, giving each student two that do NOT match and that they did NOT write. Have students take turns reading one card. Whoever has the match answers by reading their card.

 Play a circle game similar to Grandmother's Trunk, where one person makes a statement, the next person repeats that statement and adds one of his own, the third person repeats the first two statements and then adds one of his own and so on, until everyone in the circle has had a turn. For this game, make statements about an Earth-friendly practice. (Ex. 1: I made a bird feeder. 2: She made a bird feeder, and I put on a sweatshirt to keep warm. 3: She made a bird feeder, he put on a sweatshirt and I turned off the TV when I left the room.) If you have a large group, try making several smaller circles of five to eight children each.

Holidays & Seasonal Celebrations, Issue 8, Teaching & Learning Co. © 1997, Carthage, IL 62321

To Have a Dream

January 15th is the birthday of Dr. Martin Luther King, Jr., a man honored for his peaceful efforts to obtain equal political, social, and economic rights for all groups.

Dr. King

Display a picture of Dr. Martin Luther King, Jr. or share pictures from a book. Ask the children if they know who he is. Have them contribute any ideas about why he is famous. Briefly discuss the term *rights* and prompt them for ideas as to what kinds of rights people in the United States have. Explain that Dr. King's dream or hope was that all people would be able to have the same rights. Ask the children for their thoughts on whether or not this dream has become a reality.

Differences

Introduce the concept of "different, but the same" by using inanimate objects, such as two pillows. Encourage the children to explain how they can simultaneously be different and the same. Have them search throughout the room for other objects that are also the same yet different and share their discoveries with the class. Relate the same idea to individuals in the class. Have them contribute observations about physical differences, even though they are all children.

Peaceful Progress

Explain to the children that Dr. King worked to change laws in peaceful ways such as speeches and marches. He was awarded the Nobel Peace Prize for his peaceful efforts towards change. Provide the children with paper, markers and scissors. Have them each create their own peace prize. Staple crepe paper streamers to each of their designs. Use safety pins to attach the peace prizes onto their chests to wear in honor of Dr. Martin Luther King, Jr.

Lights, Camera, Action

Invite individual children to role-play peaceful solutions to familiar situations. Suggestions: Two children wanting to play with the same toy. Someone borrowing a favorite toy, then losing it or breaking it. Someone being unkind to a sister, brother or friend.

by Marie E. Cecchini

Public Speaking

Share pictures of Dr. Martin Luther King, Jr. and others giving speeches from a *podium* or *lectern*. Introduce these words. Explore reasons why a speaker might use one. Have the children assist you in constructing a lectern from a cardboard box and brown paper. Tape a yardstick to the lectern for a microphone. Invite the children to take turns at the lectern and give a short speech about something they did that expressed kindness and fairness to another person.

If I Could

Ask the children to think about things they would like to do to make the world a better place for everyone to live. Provide them with paper and markers to make posters about Dr. Martin Luther King, Jr. or about the things they would like to do. Staple each poster to a sturdy cardboard stick. Have them march in their own peace parade, carrying their posters for a better world.

Dr. Martin Luther King, Jr.

Dr. Martin Luther King, Jr. had a special dream
(Put palms of hands together and rest cheek on them.)
That he wanted to share with others.
(Spread out arms.)
He wanted people to talk—not scream—
(Speak softly, cover ears on "scream.")
And all be sisters and brothers.
(Join hands with friends.)

All People

Share the following poem with your students and talk about what the last two lines mean.

Happy Birthday, Martin

Happy birthday, dear Martin.
Happy birthday to you.
We're learning to celebrate
All people, too.

Holidays & Seasonal Celebrations, Issue 8, Teaching & Learning Co. © 1997, Carthage, IL 62321

Cooking with Kids

Hearts Delight

Ingredients:

    2 large boxes of red gelatin
    2 pints whipping cream
    2 cans crushed pineapple (drained)

Have the children make the gelatin as directed on the package. You may wish to use the pineapple juice in place of water. Allow the gelatin to partially set. Whip the cream. Combine the pineapple, whipped cream and gelatin. Stir until well mixed. Refrigerate about an hour. Spoon into small paper cups and enjoy!

Crackers with Heart

Ingredients:

snack crackers	frosting (or cream cheese)
red food coloring	large marshmallows
cinnamon hearts	tongue depressor sticks

Give each student a snack cracker. Add a couple drops of red food coloring to the frosting or cream cheese; stir until blended. Have the students use a stick to spread some frosting or cream cheese over their cracker. Place a big marshmallow on top of the frosting. Add a little more frosting to the top of the marshmallow. Stick a cinnamon heart on top.

Happy Hearts

Ingredients:

1 cup butter	1 cup sugar
1 egg	3 T. milk
1 tsp. vanilla extract	3 cups flour
1 1/2 tsp. baking powder	1/2 tsp. salt
vanilla frosting	cinnamon hearts
red shoestring licorice	icing tube
heart-shaped cookie cutter	

Cream butter and sugar together in medium-size mixing bowl. Beat in egg, vanilla and milk. Stir in flour, baking powder and salt until well mixed. Preheat oven to 400°F. Roll out dough, 1/3 at a time, on a floured surface to 1/8" thickness. Using cookie cutter, cut into heart shapes. Place 1" apart on ungreased baking sheets. Bake for 5-8 minutes (until golden brown).

Once cookies have cooled, fill icing tube with frosting and have children outline the inside of their cookie heart. Have them put a small squirt of icing where the eyes, nose and mouth would go. Place a cinnamon heart on the two spots for the eyes and for the nose. Cut 1" pieces of licorice and put on the frosting spots for the mouth and eyebrows. Have a heart and enjoy!

by Teresa E. Culpeper

Paddy's Parfaits

Ingredients:

green gelatin
pistachio-flavored instant pudding
clear plastic glasses

1 pint whipping cream
green gummi candy

Have students make up the gelatin according to the package directions. (You may want to make this the day before you plan to use it.) Refrigerate until set. Make up the pudding according to package directions. Whip the cream. Put a couple of spoonfuls of gelatin in each glass. Add a couple of spoonfuls of pudding on top. Place a spoonful of whipped cream on top of the pudding. Top it off with a green gummi candy. Enjoy!

Hoppy's Happy Salad

Ingredients:

red and green leaf lettuce
1 cup raisins
1 1/2 cups mini marshmallows
1/4 cup orange juice
1 1/4 cups light salad dressing

2 medium carrots (shredded)
3/4 cup chopped walnuts
2 medium apples (chopped)
1/4 cup honey

Have students wash the lettuce and tear into bite-size pieces. Shred carrots; peel and chop apple into bite-size chunks. Mix lettuce, carrots, raisins, walnuts, marshmallows and apples together. In separate bowl, mix together orange juice, honey and dressing. Pour over salad and toss until well blended. Serve up and nibble away!

Shamus' Shanty

Ingredients:

limeade
your favorite ice cream
green maraschino cherries
clear plastic glasses, straws and spoons

Scoop a couple of spoonfuls of ice cream into each glass. Fill glass with limeade. Top with a maraschino cherry. Top of the mornin' to you! (You can substitute ginger ale or lemon-lime soda for the limeade, but my students enjoyed the refreshing taste of the limeade.)

Bunny Ears

Ingredients:

1/2 banana per student (cut in half lengthwise)
chocolate sauce
2 pints whipping cream
2 white cake mixes
9" x 13" pans
chocolate sprinkles

Prepare cake mixes according to package directions. Set aside until cool. Whip cream; slice bananas in half lengthwise. Cut cake in lengths about 2" wide. Each student receives one length of cake on a small plate. Cut each length in half widthwise (so student has two pieces of cake). Trim the top end of each piece slightly so they look like rabbits ears. Place a banana slice on each "ear." Dribble chocolate sauce over the entire ear. Spoon whipped cream on top.

Warming Up with Fingerplays

January Snow

All night long the snowflakes fell.
(Wiggle fingers downward.)

They didn't make a sound!
(Put index finger to lips.)

When they came, I cannot tell,
(Shake head back and forth and shrug.)

But they covered all the ground!
(Indicate with arms.)

by Judy Wolfman

A Snowy Day

These are the snowflakes as they fall.
(Flutter fingers downward.)

Here is the snowman, straight and tall.
(Put up index finger on right hand.)

Here is the sun at the end of the day.
(Use thumb and forefinger of left hand and put over the index finger.)

Now the snowman melts away.
(Slowly put down index finger.)

by Judy Wolfman

Let's Warm Up!

We're cold! We're cold! We've been out in a storm!
(Cross arms and shiver.)

Let's run back inside so we can get warm!
(Pretend to run.)

Off come our mittens. Pull your boots—really try!
(Pull off "mittens" and "boots.")

Now take your coat off to hang up and dry.
(Pretend to take off coat.)

The wood in our fireplace goes snap! pop!
and crack!
(Make loud noises.)

First warm your hands, and then warm your back.
(Hold out hands; then turn around.)

Now for some good warm soup, and then—
(Pretend to eat soup.)

Back out to play in the snow again!
(Clap hands.)

by Bonnie Compton Hanson

Holidays & Seasonal Celebrations, Issue 8, Teaching & Learning Co. © 1997, Carthage, IL 62321

Tu B'Shvat
The New Year of the Trees

Tu B'Shvat

Tu B'Shvat is a Jewish holiday that is celebrated in January or February. Its name means "the fifteenth of Shvat." Shvat is the fifth month in the Jewish calendar.

Tu B'Shvat is the New Year of the Trees. This holiday falls during the cold winter months in most of North America. In Israel, however, it marks the beginning of spring. At this time, almond trees are in bloom throughout Israel. Many people celebrate by planting trees.

In America, Tu B'Shvat has become a time to celebrate the environment. Some people observe the holiday with a special meal. They have readings, songs and prayers about nature. All kinds of fruits are eaten, especially those that grow in Israel.

Bean Tree

Purchase dry lentils, split peas, navy beans, kidney beans and any other large beans or seeds you can find. Provide each child with glue, beans and a sheet of stiff cardboard. Have students glue the beans onto the cardboard in the shape of a tree. They can use different colors for the trunk, the leaves and flowers. Keep the trees flat and allow them to dry thoroughly before displaying them in the classroom.

by Katy Z. Allen and Gabi Mezger

The Uses of Trees

Challenge students to think of the many ways in which trees are useful. With older students, have small groups work cooperatively to make lists and then share their ideas while you write them on the board. Have younger students simply suggest ideas. Remind students to think of uses in the natural world (such as providing places for birds' nests), as well as uses for people. How many ideas can they think of? Afterward, have each student pick one or two uses and draw a picture to illustrate it. Create a bulletin board with the title "The Uses of Trees."

The Lorax

Read the Dr. Seuss book *The Lorax,* or show the video. Afterward, discuss the story. Ask the following questions: Why do you think Dr. Seuss wrote this story? Do you think that what happened in this story could happen to our world? What can children do to help protect trees?

All Kinds of Fruits

Provide students with a variety of fruits with which they might not be familiar, such as carob, figs, dates, almonds, pomegranates, star fruit or whatever is available in your local supermarket. Take a survey to find out which fruits are the most popular.

Holidays & Seasonal Celebrations, Issue 8, Teaching & Learning Co. © 1997, Carthage, IL 62321

Fruit People

Turn the fruit into people or animals. Give them eyes, mouths and noses.
Give them arms and legs. Color them.

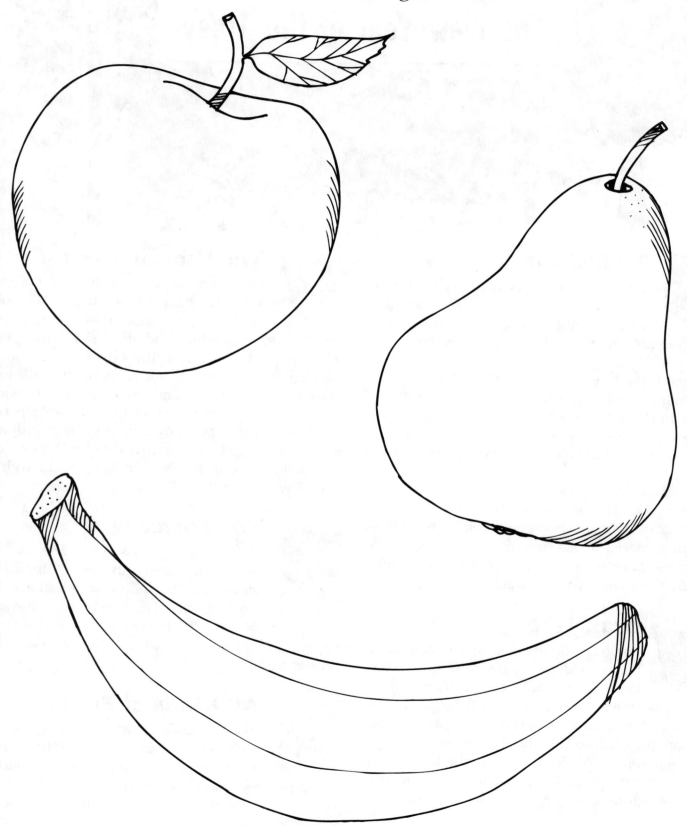

Math in Hebrew

The language of Israel is Hebrew. Hebrew is read from left to right. It has a different alphabet. In Hebrew, letters are also numbers. Below are 10 Hebrew letters and the numbers they equal.

6 = ו   1 = א

7 = ז   2 = ב

8 = ח   3 = ג

9 = ט   4 = ד

10 = י   5 = ה

Try to do math in Hebrew. Add or subtract. Write the answer with regular numbers.

ו
+ ז
___

ב
+ ח
___

א
+ ג
___

ט
- ה
___

ח
- ז
___

י
- א
___

Happy Birthday, Benjamin Franklin!

Just one of Benjamin Franklin's accomplishments would be enough to make him famous; it's amazing how many things this man invented and the achievements he made. He called himself a printer; however, his talents included that of a writer, diplomat, scientist, inventor, philosopher, educator and public servant.

Benjamin Franklin was born in Boston, Massachusetts, on January 17, 1706. He was the 15th child in a family of 17. His father, from England, was a poor soap and candle maker. Since education was expensive, Benjamin did not have much formal schooling after the age of 10.

In 1732, Franklin published his most famous work, *The Poor Richard's Almanac*. The almanac was a calendar and weather forecast for the year and contained jokes and proverbs. Franklin published under the pen name of Richard Saunders. Two famous proverbs of Poor Richard were "Early to bed, early to rise makes a man healthy, wealthy and wise" and "A rotten apple spoils his companions." Both the almanac and a newspaper

he helped publish sold well. Franklin set up numerous print shops in other colonies and became wealthy enough to retire from business at the age of 42.

Benjamin Franklin was an active inventor throughout his adult years. He invented the Franklin Stove, which helped heat drafty homes. His most important work was done with electricity. He studied works of the European scientists where they stored electricity in special tubes. He tried these experiments himself and later published a book about electricity.

He conducted a famous experiment with his son, William, that intrigues all students. Franklin realized that lightning was a discharge of electricity from the clouds. The father-son team went out to a meadow and flew a kite during a thunderstorm. He attached a metal key to the bottom of the string. A charge of electricity went down the wet string, and as he placed his knuckle to the key, he saw an electrical spark. This proved his theory that lightning is electricity. He followed up this experiment

by inventing the lightning rod to protect buildings from lightning bolts.

Benjamin Franklin organized a postal system. Before stamps were used, a person would collect his mail at the post office and pay for it. Because of unclaimed mail, money was lost. Franklin decided to print the names of people who had mail awaiting them. He set up a bookkeeping system. In 1753, Franklin was made Deputy Postmaster General for all the colonies. Mail was carried by stagecoach across the country; however, Franklin devised many ways to improve the system.

Franklin was an important statesman. He signed four important documents: the Declaration of Independence (1776), the Treaty of Alliance with France (1778), the Treaty of Paris (1783) and the Constitution (1787). He died on April 17, 1790. Today, look for Benjamin Franklin's picture on the U.S. $100 bill.

Try a few of the following classroom activities with your students as you study this famous man in the month of January.

by Tania Kourempis-Cowling

Holidays & Seasonal Celebrations, Issue 8, Teaching & Learning Co. © 1997, Carthage, IL 62321

Deliver the Mail

Print each consonant on the front of an envelope. Give an envelope to each child in the classroom. Choose one child to be the letter carrier. This person carries a paper sack full of cards with pictures on them. The letter carrier pulls out a picture and tries to find the student with the correct envelope—the beginning sound of the object in the picture should match the letter on the envelope. Variations could be matching capital letters with lowercase; matching colors, shapes or numerals with dots on a card and so on.

Paper Plate Kite

Glue strips of crepe paper to one side of a paper plate. Tie a yarn handle to the opposite side of the plate. Let the students hold on to the yarn handle and run with the kite to make it fly. This is a great art project, as the children color and decorate the plates, and then take them outdoors for a fun running and flying experience.

Kite Picture

Copy a drawing of Benjamin Franklin. Cut out the drawing and glue it onto light blue construction paper. Make a kite out of colorful paper, fabric or wallpaper. Glue this onto the paper, along with string, to make a kite picture. Draw dark clouds and lightning bolts. Don't forget to attach a cut-out key shape.

Poor Richard's Proverbs

Match the beginning of the proverb with its ending by placing the correct letter in the blank.

_____ An apple a day

_____ A bird in the hand

_____ Little strokes fell

_____ Look before

_____ Early to bed, early to rise

_____ An ounce of prevention

a. is worth two in the bush.

b. great oaks.

c. is worth a pound of cure.

d. keeps the doctor away.

e. you leap.

f. makes a man healthy, wealthy and wise.

National Handwriting Day
January 23

Practice writing *welcome* in different languages from other countries. See if you can copy the following writing samples. Get a taste of handwriting from around the world!

Korean 환영 합니다

Hebrew אֶכֶב רָיוּךְ

English Welcome

Russian Добро́ пожа́ловать

Arabic أَهْلاً وسَهْلاً

Chinese 歡 迎

Japanese ようこそ

by Donna L. Clovis

Holidays & Seasonal Celebrations, Issue 8, Teaching & Learning Co. © 1997, Carthage, IL 62321

Mardi Gras

In the South, just say the words *Mardi Gras* and children, as well as adults, think of fun, fantasy, mystery and merriment. Explore the meaning and history behind the yearly carnival celebration.

The Beginning of Mardi Gras

Mardi Gras, or Carnival as it is sometimes called, is the celebration time of Christians before the season of Lent. The Christians were once required by their church to fast from meat, eggs and dairy products during the Lent period before Easter. The word *carnival* comes from the Latin words that mean "the taking away of meat." Therefore, before this fasting period began, the people celebrated heartily by indulging in rich foods, dance and masquerade.

Mardi Gras is celebrated all over the world. Its name is different in different countries. For example, the Germans call it *Fasching* and the Polish call it *Zapusty*.

Calendar Calculations

Mardi Gras is calculated by use of the Gregorian calendar and lunar aspects, as well. Easter occurs on the first Sunday after the first full moon, after the vernal equinox (relating to spring, March 23). That is why the date is different from year to year. The 40 days before Easter are called Lent. The last day before Lent is called Fat Tuesday, the most famous day of the Mardi Gras celebration. The festivities go on for a week or two prior to Fat Tuesday. The last day before Lent (Fat Tuesday) will be February 11, 1997, and Easter falls on March 30, 1997. Therefore, Mardi Gras starts very early in February.

Mardi Gras Today

Mardi Gras is a time of merriment for all and is celebrated throughout the United States. However, big parades are seen and broadcast on television throughout Mobile, Alabama; New Orleans, Louisiana, and other towns along the Gulf Coast, even into the panhandle of Florida. Everyone is busy during this holiday season. Parade floats are constructed, costumes are sewn, trinkets are manufactured, cakes are baked and children are engaged in decorating their schools and the community with their artwork.

King Cakes

King Cakes are found in bakeries beginning on January 6 (Epiphany), officially starting the Mardi Gras season. In European countries, the Feast of Epiphany is celebrated to honor the coming of the Wise Men bearing gifts to the Christ Child. The baking of King Cakes has long been a custom. Europeans bake an almond inside, and the person who receives it in their piece of cake must portray one of the Magi, also receiving good luck. Today, Americans put a small plastic baby figurine inside, and the person receiving it must bake or bring the next King Cake to the parties. King Cakes are oval, ringed danish cakes filled with fruits and sweets. They are topped with icing in the royal colors of Mardi Gras—purple (justice), green (faith) and gold (power). King Cake season ends on Fat Tuesday, the day before Lent.

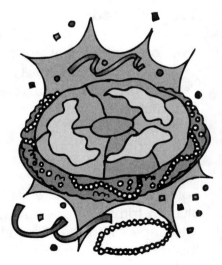

by Tania K. Cowling

Holidays & Seasonal Celebrations, Issue 8, Teaching & Learning Co. © 1997, Carthage, IL 62321

Celebrating in the Classroom

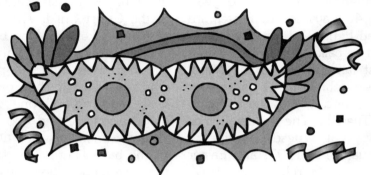

Mardi Gras Masks

Students can make their own masquerade masks from poster board. Cut out a mask shape. Collect decorating trims in the festive colors of purple, green and yellow (gold). Glue on sequins, feathers, glitter, lace and so on. Attach a piece of elastic to the back of the mask with a stapler so it will fit the child's head.

Toy Floats

Gather several boxes of different sizes (jewelry boxes are perfect for this project). Cover these with tissue or construction paper in Mardi Gras colors. Glue the boxes together to make a float replica. Add decorative trims, make paper flags, use stickers, attach plastic people or animals—all to make an authentic-looking parade float. Place the children's floats along a shelf to make a street parade display.

King Puppets

You will need:

- 1 shoulder pad (removed from an old sweater or blouse; colored fabric ones are best)
- round Styrofoam™ ball or Ping-Pong™ ball
- tacky glue or low temperature glue gun
- toothpick
- paint and markers
- lace, rickrack, trims, etc.
- chenille strips

Fold the shoulder pad ends to meet in the center. Glue these together to look like a robe. You can also glue on trims, buttons and so on to make the character. Paint facial features onto the round ball. Poke a toothpick into the ball and then insert this head into the top edge of the shoulder pad puppet. Glue this into place. Arms can be made by wrapping chenille strips (pipe cleaners) around the head portion and shaping these into arms. The child can then place their finger into the bottom edge of the shoulder pad to manipulate their puppet's actions.

24

King Cupcakes

Make cupcakes for the class according to package directions. This could be a class cooking project or brought in from home. The fun part is making the royal icing. Place confectioner's sugar into three bowls. Moisten the sugar slightly with water to make a frosting consistency. Add drops of food coloring to make Mardi Gras colors.

> Purple—drops of red and blue
> Green—drops of yellow and blue
> Yellow—drops of yellow

Spread this thin icing on top of each cake. Add multicolored sprinkles for a festive look.

Junk Jug Shaker

Make a parade even more festive by creating rattling sounds to go with the music. A homemade instrument that could add these sounds would be a "junk jug shaker." Each child will need an empty milk or juice jug with a handle. Then have fun collecting objects to place inside for noises. Items like wooden beads, jingle bells, dried beans, pennies, pebbles and so on could be used. Apply glue to the inside of the jug lid before screwing it into place. Have the children hold the jug by its handle and shake it up and down as they march around the room.

Bead Necklaces

There are two types of homemade necklaces that can easily be made in the classroom. You can make a clay mixture and roll beads, or string colorful pasta. Here is one recipe for salt dough (there are many others in art books). Mix 1 cup salt, $1/2$ cup cornstarch and $3/4$ cup water in a pan. Stir these ingredients over low heat. After the mixture has thickened, in about three minutes or so, place it onto waxed paper. Let the dough cool slightly and then proceed to knead it until smooth. Roll the dough into small balls and push a plastic straw through the center to make a threading hole. Allow the beads to air dry thoroughly.

Optional: Purchase multicolored pasta or tint regular pasta by using food coloring. Dip the pasta into a bowl containing water, food coloring and a teaspoon of rubbing alcohol. Leave the pasta in this mixture only long enough for the pasta to tint, and then quickly remove it to air dry on waxed paper. Thread the beads or pasta onto a length of yarn. Tie the ends together after measuring around the child's head for size.

Mardi Gras Resources

Coasting Through Mardi Gras—A Guide to Carnival Along the Gulf Coast by Judy Barnes, Jolane Edwards, Carolyn Lee Goodloe and Laurel Wilson. Copies can be obtained by writing to: Coasting, P.O. Box 25, Point Clear, AL 36564

Arthur Hardy's Mardi Gras Guide ($6.50). Write to: P.O. Box 19500, New Orleans, LA 70179

Tourist Information: Call (504) 566-5005
Computer Advice: http://www.nawlins.com

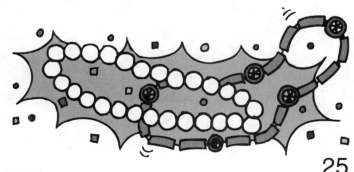

February
Children's Dental Health Month

by Jo Jo Cavalline and Jo Anne O'Donnell

Dental health is a very important part of a child's development. To encourage good dental health, discuss the proper care of teeth and the importance of seeing a dentist. Try the following activities during Children's Dental Health Month.

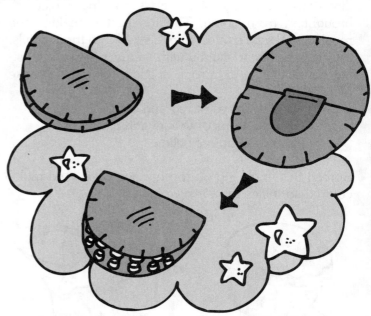

Davey Dentist's Mouth

Materials:
- paper plate (not Styrofoam™)
- red construction paper
- 32 white miniature marshmallows
- glue
- scissors

Fold the paper plate in half to create a mouth shape; then open it up again. Cut a tongue from the red construction paper, 3 1/2" x 2 1/2", and round one end. Glue the tongue in the center of the paper plate. Glue 16 marshmallows around the top of the plate and 16 marshmallows around the bottom of the plate for teeth. Have the children review their dental health lessons by making Davey Dentist's mouth open and shut like a puppet.

Toothbrush

Materials:
- poster board, 15" x 3"
- 30 foam packaging pieces
- glue
- scissors

Round the edges of the poster board as shown. Glue the foam pieces on one end of the poster board to form the bristles of the toothbrush.

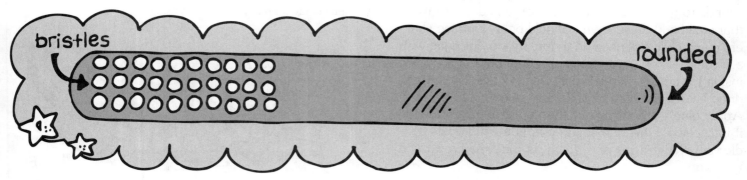

bristles

rounded

Holidays & Seasonal Celebrations, Issue 8, Teaching & Learning Co. © 1997, Carthage, IL 62321

Tooth Poem

When I smile I want you to see
My teeth as white as they can be.
I brush them morning, noon and night
So they will stay shiny and bright!

Brush Your Teeth Song

(To the tune of "Row, Row, Row Your Boat")

Brush, brush, brush your teeth,
  (Use index finger and pretend to brush teeth.)
Brush them every day.
  (Continue to brush.)
Brush them up and down and 'round.
  (Brush as stated.)
Brush in every way!
  (Brush in all directions.)

by Judy Wolfman

Bulletin Board

Have the children bring in pictures of people show-ing their teeth when they are smiling. The pictures can be from magazines, newspapers, food containers or from their family albums. The title of your bulletin board could be "Smile and the World Smiles with You" or "Smile–It's Contagious" The bulletin board will generate discussion and smiles.

Riddle: What is the longest word in the dictionary?

Smiles. There is a mile between the two Ss!

Holidays & Seasonal Celebrations, Issue 8, Teaching & Learning Co. © 1997, Carthage, IL 62321

It's Groundhog Day

The Groundhog

The groundhog comes out of the ground.
> *(With thumb and forefinger of left hand, make a circle.
> Stick forefinger of right hand through it.)*

First he looks up; then he looks down.
> *(Stick finger way up, then bring it down.)*

If he sees his shadow, he runs back inside
> *(Quickly bring finger out.)*

For six more weeks, where he stays and hides.
> *(Put finger behind back.)*

by Judy Wolfman

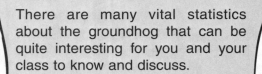

There are many vital statistics about the groundhog that can be quite interesting for you and your class to know and discuss.

Common Name: groundhog or woodchuck

Family: They are members of the rodent family and the largest species of the squirrel family. They are also related to gophers, which are also called prairie dogs and beavers.

Average Weight: Around 10-15 pounds

Average Length: 1 to 1 1/2 feet long

Coloration: Brownish-black with yellow highlights

Life Span: About six years in the wild and between 10-15 years in captivity

Range: The types we see live in the eastern United States and in southern and eastern Canada.

Population: There is a large amount of these animals. There's as many woodchucks as there are raccoons and opossums, mostly in the rural areas rather than the city.

"To see or not to see its shadow" is the question of the day on February 2. It's officially Groundhog Day when this small creature predicts the upcoming seasonal weather. The legend states that if the groundhog comes out of his burrow and sees his shadow, we're in for six more weeks of winter. If no shadow is seen, spring is on its way.

Many years ago in England, Scotland and Germany, the folk belief was that hibernating animals would awaken in mid-winter to check the weather and decide whether to go back to sleep or stay up for spring. February 2 seemed to be the day of choice. This custom was brought to the United States by German immigrants in the late 1800s. They settled in an area of Pennsylvania called Punxsutawney, which is 100 miles northeast of Pittsburgh.

Punxsutawney Phil is the world's most famous groundhog. He is the one that television networks and national publications arrange to see and film. Phil lives the life of the rich and famous as he resides in a custom-designed den at the Punxsutawney, Pennsylvania, library. He is a tourist attraction, and once a year he treks up to Gobbler's Knob for the shadow ritual, which has been a tradition since 1886. If you need more information about famous Phil, use the following sources to find out what you want to know.

The Punxsutawney Chamber of Commerce 1-800-752-PHIL

Phil's Fan Club ($7.50 a year)
Punxsutawney Groundhog Club
Chamber of Commerce
124 W. Mahoning Street
Punxsutawney, PA 15767

A gift catalog of custom sourvenirs is also available through the Chamber of Commerce.

Computer Web Site:
http.//www.groundhog.org

by **Tania K. Cowling**

Holidays & Seasonal Celebrations, Issue 8, Teaching & Learning Co. © 1997, Carthage, IL 62321

Lunch Bag Puppet

Duplicate copies of the groundhog above. Have the children color and decorate it. Cut out the two pieces and glue them onto the lunch bag to make a puppet. Then have children place their hands into the bags to manipulate the puppets.

Groundhog Art

Tell the children to pretend they are groundhogs. You have awakened and are looking outside your burrow. What do you see?

Have students draw and color a picture. Share each picture with the class.

Shadow Fun

Use flashlights or spotlights to play these games.

1. Pick a spot on the wall or floor. Guess where to place your finger so that the shadow touches the spot.
2. Use various objects to create shadows. Does the object always cast the same shadow?
3. Make a big shadow. Make a small shadow. (Move close to or far from the light to create these images.)
4. Make your own shadow dance, wave, twirl around, fall down, jump and so on.

Shadow Partners

Have children pick a partner and pretend to be each other's shadow. The children face one another. One child moves, making obvious motions, while the other child tries to mirror what the first one is doing. Take turns trying both roles.

Pop-Up Puppet

Your students can make pop-up puppets using paper cups and tongue depressors. The paper or foam cups can be decorated with markers and stickers. On a tongue depressor, the children can draw the face of a groundhog. Cut a slit in the bottom of the cup and insert the stick. The children can raise or lower the groundhog by pushing the depressor up and down from under the cup.

Holidays & Seasonal Celebrations, Issue 8, Teaching & Learning Co. © 1997, Carthage, IL 62321

Groundhog Day Bulletin Board

Ode to the Forecaster

Groundhog, Groundhog,
Please tell us what to do.
Should we wax our sleds?
Or will the sky be blue?

Groundhog, Groundhog,
Tell us what to do.
Please tell us, Groundhog,
We're counting on you!

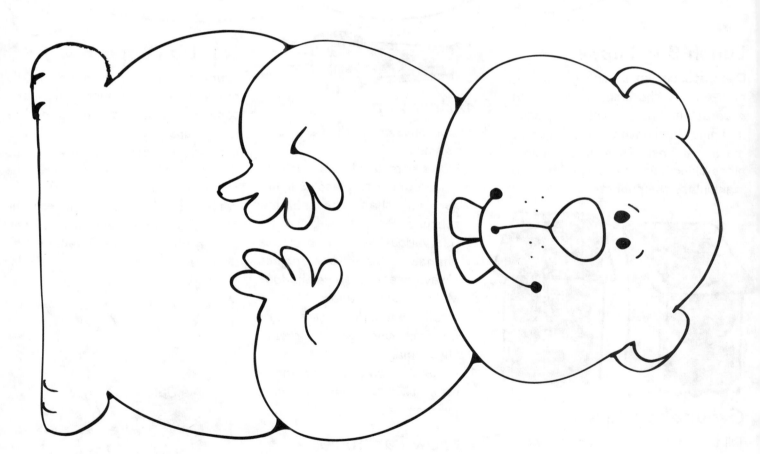

Make groundhog puppets on a stick. Use while reciting the poem. On February 2, when the groundhog makes his prediction, write his reply in rhyme. Example: No, no there won't be snow.

Right into spring we go!

You can also use this as a bulletin board activity as shown. Give each child a groundhog and let him or her predict if the groundhog will indeed see his shadow.

by Jo Jo Cavalline and Jo Anne O'Donnell

Holidays & Seasonal Celebrations, Issue 8, Teaching & Learning Co. © 1997, Carthage, IL 62321

Quick, grease the griddle! Pancake Day is February 2, if you happen to live in France. In England, Shrove Tuesday is the day for flapjack festivities. In the U.S., there is a whole week for celebration. National Pancake Week is February 16-22. Pancake Day in France brings opportunities for a year's worth of good luck. Grown-ups challenge themselves to toss pancakes in the air and catch them in a pan, while holding a coin in the other hand. Children gain good luck by finding a thread baked into a pancake. Festivities in England include pancake races and pancake-eating contests.

Chances are that you would not choose to have pancakes flying and skillets waving in your classroom, nor would you wish to send your students home with stomachaches, but Pancake Day can still be fun. Try these activities for a fun-filled Pancake Day.

by Gloria Trabacca

Pancake Mix Measuring

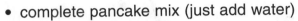

- complete pancake mix (just add water)
- zippered plastic bags
- measuring cups and spoons
- 1 penny for each child
- large bowl

Pour the pancake mix into a large bowl and provide measuring cups for children to use to fill their own bags. Tell them how many cups of mix to place in their bags.

For older children, make this activity more challenging by removing the one-cup measure and replacing it with assorted sizes of measuring cups and spoons. Provide them with measurement equivalents, such as 3 tsp. = 1 T. and 16 T. = 1 cup.

Tape a penny to the Good Luck card (directions provided on the following page), attach the card to the bag of pancake mix and have children take them home and share the story of Pancake Day with their families.

Pancake Catch

- smallest size plastic cups
- 18" lengths of string (one per child)
- quarter-size tagboard "pancakes"
- tape

Have students cut out a tagboard pancake. Tape the pancake to one end of a length of string. Tape the other end of the string to the inside bottom of the paper cup. Have fun trying to flip the pancake into the paper cup "pan."

31

Pancake Good Luck Cards

Make copies of the card pattern below. Provide tan crayons and brightly colored yarn. Punch holes where marked around the edges of the cover page, and at the top of the inside page. Students may first color their cards, and then lace yarn around the cover page. Have students begin and end the lacing at the top of the pan-cake. The final few stitches should pass through both pieces of paper to attach the front and back of the card. Or cards may be stapled at the top. In this case, omit holes from the second page of the card. Send Good Luck cards home with a pancake mix gift.

In France, today is Pancake Day,
with food to eat and games to play.
They flip a pancake in the air
and catch it if they may.
If they catch it, then good luck
will be theirs all year through.
So, I'm bringing you this card,
and you can try for good luck, too!

Books to Read

Pancakes for Breakfast by Tomie de Paola. Harcourt Brace Jovanovich, 1978.

The Pancake by Anita Lobel. Greenwillow Books, 1978.

Celebrate

Halfway Day

February 4th is Halfway Day, the day when we are halfway through winter.
Celebrate by "searching for the sun."

"Sun"glasses

Make "sun"glasses out of paper plates, paint, glitter and yarn. (Remember to make these a day ahead so they can be worn on Halfway Day.)

- paper plate halves with eyeholes precut
- yellow and orange paint
- gold glitter
- yarn in complementary colors

Provide each student with a paper plate half. They can first cut "rays," and then paint their sun bright orange and yellow. If desired, gold glitter may be sprinkled on the wet paint to help the sun shine! Punch one hole in either side of the sunglasses, thread with yarn and tie to fit each child.

by Gloria Trabacca

Holidays & Seasonal Celebrations, Issue 8, Teaching & Learning Co. © 1997, Carthage, IL 62321

You Are My Sunshine

Sit in a circle and sing "You Are My Sunshine." Take turns choosing emotion and color words to substitute for *happy* and *gray*.

Seashell Hunt

Hide two or three sizes of seashell macaroni in your classroom and have a treasure hunt. Assign a number value to each size. Who has the most shells? Who has the least? Whose shells have the most or least value? Have the class choose different number values. Which answers will change? Whose shells have the most/least value now?

Beach Collage

- construction paper
- sand
- seashell pasta
- crayons
- glue

Make a beach collage, starting with crayons and torn paper. Add sand and seashell pasta to make a beautiful beach to take home.

Picnic at the Beach

Spread out beach blankets and have a sunny day picnic. Slice oranges into sunshine circles or serve pineapple rings with pretzel stick rays.

Sandcastles

Put damp sand in your water table, along with pails, shovels and various containers for making sandcastles (margarine tubs, yogurt cups, etc.). Challenge students to build a two-story castle or a tunnel that doesn't collapse.

Holidays & Seasonal Celebrations, Issue 8, Teaching & Learning Co. © 1997, Carthage, IL 62321

HAPPY BIRTHDAY, ABE!

Abraham Lincoln's birthday is celebrated in many of the United States. Some celebrate the anniversary of his birth on February 12th, his actual birthday. Others celebrate it on the first Monday in February. Still others include Lincoln's birthday in their Presidents' Day celebration on the third Monday in February. By including a celebration of Abraham Lincoln's birthday in your February schedule, you can help students learn more about this great man.

Heads and Tails

Look at the tails side of a penny. What building is pictured? The first Lincoln head cents did not have the Lincoln Memorial pictured on them. The mem-orial was added in 1959 to celebrate the 150th anniversary of Lincoln's birthday.

Examine the picture of the Lincoln Memorial. Can children see the statue of Lincoln? The Lincoln head cent is the only United States coin with the same person pictured on the front and back.

Have the students design a coin with their picture on the front. What would be pictured on the back? What would be the value of their coin?

If I Were President

Abraham Lincoln was the sixteenth President of the United States. Two important things that he accomplished during his presidency were freeing the slaves and keeping the United Sates together. Ask students to share what they would do if they were President.

Named After Lincoln

Many buildings, parks, streets and towns are named after Abraham Lincoln. Find out if anything in your town is named for him. Use an atlas to find out how many United States cities and towns are named Lincoln. Which state is called the Land of Lincoln?

Abe's First House

When Abraham Lincoln was born, his family lived in a small, one-room log cabin. What toy used for building is named after Lincoln? Invite students to construct log cabins from this toy, or from sticks and twigs.

Abe's Coin

Ask students which United States coin has a picture of Abraham Lincoln on it. Tell them that the first Lincoln head cents were made in 1909 to celebrate the anniversary of Lincoln's 100th birthday. Give each student a penny. Show them where to find the date that tells when that penny was made. Who has the oldest penny? How many years old is it? Challenge them to find an older penny. Warn them not to take pennies out of someone's coin collection. Each time someone brings in an older penny, figure out how old it is.

Work Charades

During his lifetime, Lincoln had many different jobs. As a child and young man, he worked on his family's farm and split rails. When he left home, he worked as a ferryman, a store clerk, a postmaster, a surveyor, a lawyer, a politician and was President of the United States.

What kinds of work do the students do at home? What kinds of work would they like to do when they grow up? Invite them to act out jobs they'd like to do when they are adults. Challenge the other students to guess the job being acted out.

Suggestions for a Party

Bake gingerbread for a birthday cake. Back in Lincoln's day, gingerbread was a special treat.

Read *Abe Lincoln's Hat* by Martha Brenner. Have a hat race. Give the first person on each team a large hat stuffed with papers. That person runs to a designated place and back, then gives the hat to the second person, who does the same. If the hat falls off or any of the papers fall out, the person must stop and replace them before continuing the race. The first team to finish wins.

It's been said that Abe Lincoln would walk 20 miles to borrow a book. Celebrate his birthday with a book exchange. Ask everyone to bring in a used book.

Bibliography

Brenner, Martha. *Abe Lincoln's Hat.* Random House, New York, 1994.

Bruns, Roger. *Lincoln.* Chelsea House Publishers, New York, 1986.

D'Aulaire, Ingri, and Edgar Parin. *Abraham Lincoln.* Doubleday & Company, Inc., Garden City, New York, 1939.

Davis, Norman M. *The Complete Book of United States Coin Collecting.* Macmillan Publishing Co., Inc., New York, 1976, (pp. 45-49).

Fritz, Jean. *Just a Few Words, Mr. Lincoln.* Grosset & Dunlap, New York, 1993.

Kunhardt, Edith. *Honest Abe.* Greenwillow Books, New York, 1993.

Miller, Natalie. *The Story of the Lincoln Memorial.* Childrens Press, Chicago, 1996.

Monchieri, Lino. *Abraham Lincoln.* Silver Burdett Company, 1981.

Reed, Mort. *Cowles Complete Encyclopedia of U.S. Coins.* Cowles Book Company, Inc., New York, 1969, (pp. 97-106).

Richards, Kenneth. *The Story of the Gettysburg Address.* Childrens Press, Chicago, 1969.

The World Book Encyclopedia, vol. 12, World Book, Inc., Chicago, 1993, (pp. 329).

by Carolyn Short

Abraham Lincoln's Log Cabin

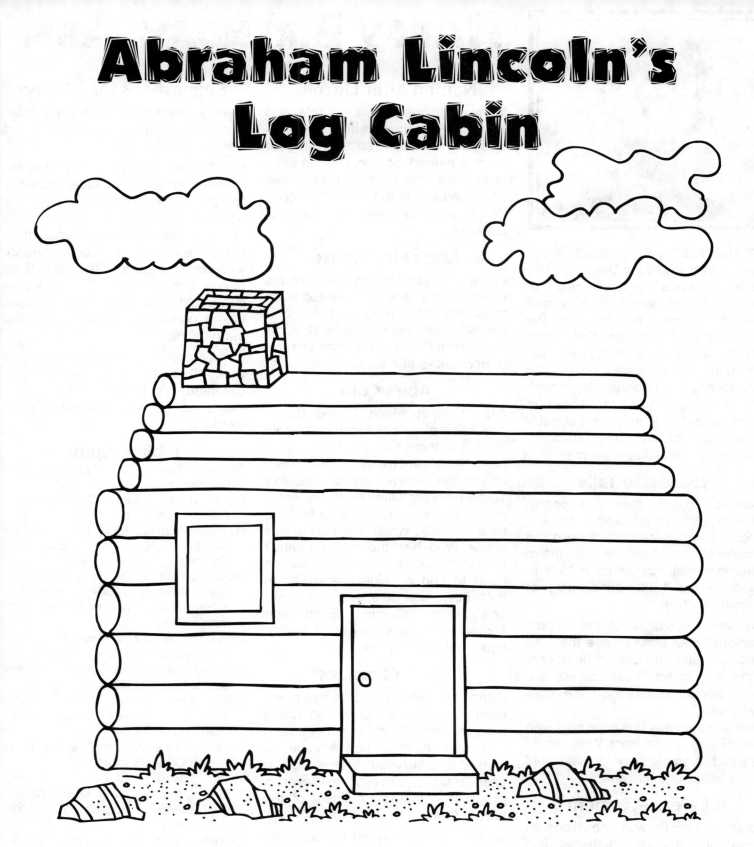

Help Abraham Lincoln cut some logs for his log cabin home. Which logs would Lincoln choose? Find the logs that tell something about Lincoln's life. Cut out the logs. Look for the places where they fit on the cabin. Then paste the logs on the cabin.
Color the picture.

by Sister Mary Yvonne Moran

Read what each log says. Find the ones that state true facts about Abraham Lincoln and his life, then color those logs. Cut the logs out and paste them in the place where they fit on the cabin.

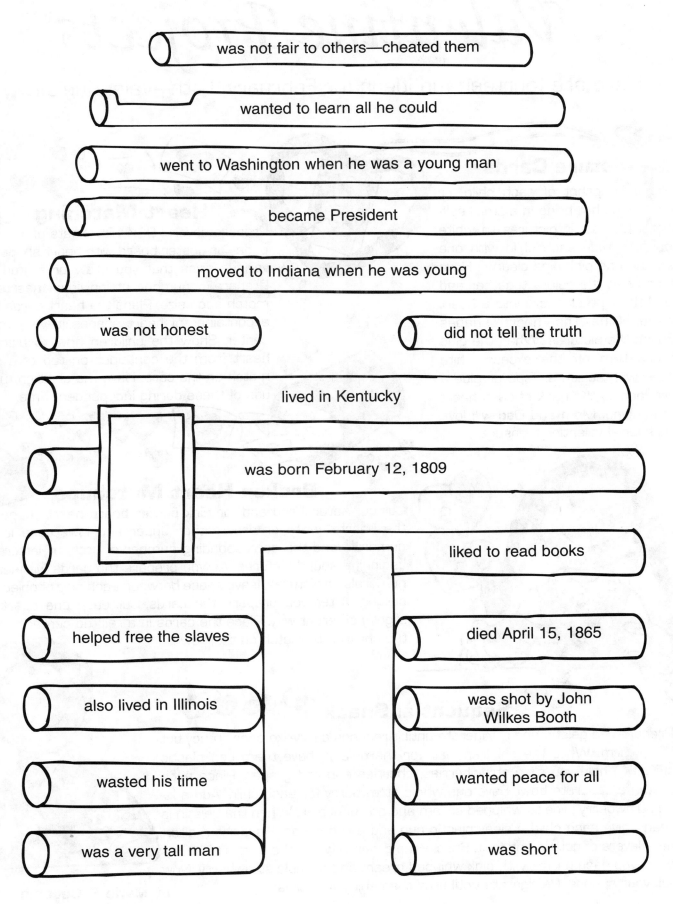

was not fair to others—cheated them

wanted to learn all he could

went to Washington when he was a young man

became President

moved to Indiana when he was young

was not honest

did not tell the truth

lived in Kentucky

was born February 12, 1809

liked to read books

helped free the slaves

died April 15, 1865

also lived in Illinois

was shot by John Wilkes Booth

wasted his time

wanted peace for all

was a very tall man

was short

14 Fabulous
Valentine Projects

Here are fourteen fun ideas for February 14th—Valentine's Day!

1 Picture Cards

Take a snapshot of each child, or have each child bring in a small self-photo. Glue their pictures to white paper. Provide each child with one red and one pink pipe cleaner. Have them twist the colors together and bend the pipe cleaners into a heart shape. Glue the heart shapes around the pictures. When the glue is dry, trim off the excess white paper with scissors. Tape or glue a yarn loop to the back of each heart for hanging. Mom and Dad will love this special valentine treasure.

2 Heart Matching

Prepare several 9" x 12" sheets of paper or poster board with heart shapes of various sizes that you draw or stamp on. Prepare a number of individual hearts to match each size. Place the heart cards and a container of heart shapes in your math center. Show the children how to place a heart from the container on top of a size match on the card. Have the children make use of these during independent time.

3 Broken Heart Matchups

Cut out several red and/or pink poster board heart shapes. On the hearts, write or draw either upper and lowercase letters, numerals and the corresponding number of dots, or letters and beginning sound pictures. As you prepare the cards with letters, numerals or pictures, leave space between each pair of objects for cutting. After you prepare the cards, cut each one apart in a slightly different way. Place the cards in a related center area for the children to match on their own.

4 Sequential Snack

Prepare red gelatin and refrigerate until it reaches a jelly-like consistency but is not firm. While the children wait for the gelatin, have them use plastic knives to help you slice strawberries, cherries and red grapes. Place each fruit in a separate bowl. Save one whole strawberry for each child. Add a little strawberry juice to whipped cream and stir until pink. When the gelatin is ready, give each child a clear plastic cup and a red spoon. Have them alternate layers of gelatin and fruit. Specify the order in which the fruit is to be layered. Top each parfait with pink whipped cream and a whole strawberry. Now lick your spoons. Refrigerate until firm; then enjoy your treat.

by Marie E. Cecchini

Holidays & Seasonal Celebrations, Issue 8, Teaching & Learning Co. © 1997, Carthage, IL 62321

Red-Letter Day

Supply each child with a white Styrofoam™ tray and a pink crayon (washable marker tends to rub off). Have them color a frame around the edges of the tray. Punch two holes at the top of each tray and thread with pink yarn for hanging. Have the children make a large V on their trays with the pink crayon. Let them trace their Vs with glue, then place red milk jug lids along their glue lines. Allow to dry. Ask them what they think the V stands for. Can they guess the sound V makes?

Heart Mobile

Cut several 3" squares of clear, self-adhesive paper. Peel the backing off of one for each child and have the children decorate the center of their squares with glitter, sequins, buttons, feathers or dried flowers. Cover their designs with a second piece of clear, self-adhesive paper and seal around the edges. Use a pattern and an ink pen to trace a heart shape around their designs. Have them cut out their hearts. Let them each make three. Punch a hole at the top of each heart, thread with a yarn length and knot. Punch three holes in a small, plastic margarine tub lid and tie the opposite ends of the yarn lengths through these holes. Tape a yarn loop to the center of the plastic lid for hanging.

Giant Heart "Cookies"

These "cookies" will look good enough to eat, but don't! Have the children cut a large heart shape from a Styrofoam™ tray. Let them paint the hearts red or pink. Allow the paint to dry; then have the children dribble glue here and there on their hearts. Sprinkle the glue with colored sugar and cake decorations or glitter and colored rice. Yum!?!

Valentine Breeze Catcher

Have the children wrap bath tissue tubes with red or pink tissue paper. Secure with tape. Let them each cut out two paper hearts and decorate with glitter. Let the glue dry, then staple the hearts to opposite sides of the tube. Tape or staple three red or pink crepe paper streamers to the bottom of the tube. Punch two holes on either side of the tube top and thread with red yarn for hanging.

Fold-Over Heart

Have the children trace and cut a large white paper heart. Provide them with cotton swabs and red and white paints. Let them dab both colors of paint onto their hearts. Before the paint dries, help them fold their hearts in half and smooth them out with flat hands. Carefully re-open the hearts. Did anyone make a new color?

Holidays & Seasonal Celebrations, Issue 8, Teaching & Learning Co. © 1997, Carthage, IL 62321

Card Carriers

10 The children will love carrying their valentine card collections home in these cute little totes. Have them cut the top off of a paper lunch bag and help them fold down the new edge. The bags should be about half their original height. Provide the children with old valentine cards, glue and scissors. Let them cut designs, pictures and words from the old cards and glue them to the outside of their bags. Cut strips of thin cardboard and have the children decorate these with markers. Staple these handles to either side of the bag top.

Heart Angels

11 For this project, each child will need one large heart, one small heart, two medium-sized hearts, a cardboard strip, a red pipe cleaner, markers, glue and tape. Place the large heart upside down (body), then glue the point of the small heart (head) to the point of the large heart. Glue the points of the medium-sized hearts (wings) to either side of the large heart. Decorate the cardboard strip with markers and staple it to the bottom of the body. Draw a face on each angel. Shape a circle at the top of the pipe cleaner and fold it forward to form a halo. Tape the bottom of the pipe cleaner to the back of the head.

"Candy" Hearts Basket

12 Twist the ends of a pipe cleaner through either side of a small, plastic produce basket to make a handle. Have the children trace and cut white Styrofoam™ hearts that are 2" to 3" across. Let them color both sides of the hearts with crayons, placing their hearts into their baskets as they are colored. Share some messages from real candy hearts, such as **yes, hug me** and **hi.** Help them use a narrow-tipped marker to write messages on their pretend candy hearts.

Heart Flowers

13 Let the children each make two heart flowers by gluing a red or pink heart to the top of two pipe cleaners and two leaf shapes to either side of each pipe cleaner. Set these on waxed paper to dry. Help them make a vase by gluing an inverted Styrofoam™ cup onto a piece of cardboard for stability. Have an adult use a ballpoint pen to carefully poke two small holes in the cup. When the glue dries, help the children push their flower stems through the holes of their "vases."

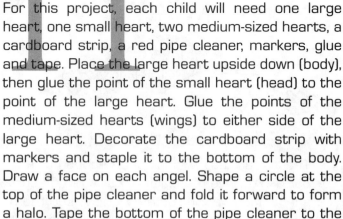

Party Place Mats

14 Have the children cut a large heart shape from white paper. Let them edge the heart with red or pink marker. Cut several vertical slits, about 1" apart, in their hearts. Provide them with red and pink paper strips to weave through the slits in their hearts.

Trim any strips that hang over the edge of the heart. Secure the ends of each strip with tape.

40

Valentine Verses

A couplet is a verse with two rhyming lines. Each line has the same number of syllables. Help the children make valentine cards featuring original couplets. The completed cards may be sent to classmates, members of their family, friends, residents at a retirement home or children in a hospital.

Before the children begin to write, introduce and reinforce rhyming words and syllables.

1. As you read stories by Dr. Seuss, have the students supply the rhyming words.

2. Present the verse, "Roses are red, violets are blue . . ." Write it on the board. Draw a line under each syllable. Clap the number of syllables in each line and count them.

3. To practice rhyming and rhythm, write the following couplets on the board. Leave blanks so the children may supply missing words. Accept any reasonable responses.

   a. Roses are red, violets are blue.
      Everything's fine when I'm with _____.

   b. Stop! Don't be a _____!
      Will you be my valentine?

   c. My heart jumps like a kangaroo,
      When I am _____ after you.

   d. I am climbing up a vine,
      _____ for my valentine.

4. Brainstorm a list of words that rhyme with *blue*. Have the students compose other endings for the "Roses are red, violets are blue" verse.

by Patricia O'Brien

Writing the Couplet

Write an opening line. Brainstorm a list of rhyming words. Write a second line that ends with a word from the list and has the same number of syllables as the first line.

Creating the Card

Materials: You will need white paper (4^1/$_2$" x 6" or 6" x 9"), felt-tipped pens, small sponges, heart-shaped stencils, paint and pencils.

Procedure: Complete the cards using any of the suggestions below.

1. To add background color, dip a sponge in paint and lightly dab it over entire surface.
2. Use the stencil and sponge to make heart patterns.
3. Carefully copy the verse onto the paper. Trace over the letters with a felt-tipped pen.
4. Add a border of hearts or colorful designs to highlight the couplet.
5. Don't forget to sign your name.

Holidays & Seasonal Celebrations, Issue 8, Teaching & Learning Co. © 1997, Carthage, IL 62321

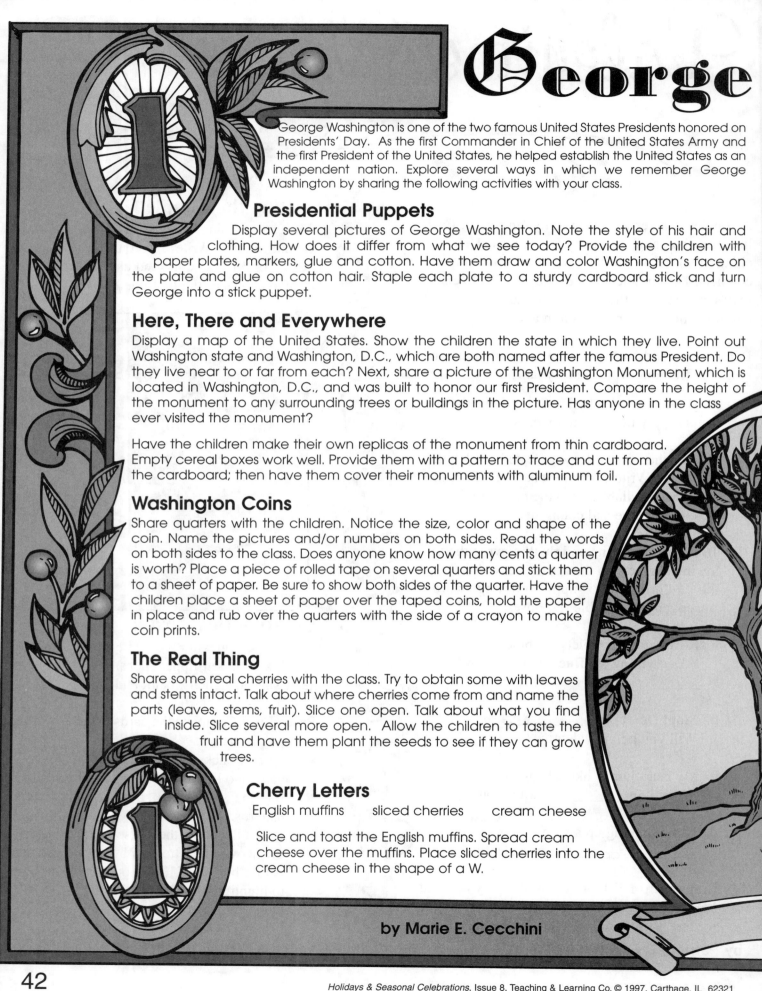

George

George Washington is one of the two famous United States Presidents honored on Presidents' Day. As the first Commander in Chief of the United States Army and the first President of the United States, he helped establish the United States as an independent nation. Explore several ways in which we remember George Washington by sharing the following activities with your class.

Presidential Puppets

Display several pictures of George Washington. Note the style of his hair and clothing. How does it differ from what we see today? Provide the children with paper plates, markers, glue and cotton. Have them draw and color Washington's face on the plate and glue on cotton hair. Staple each plate to a sturdy cardboard stick and turn George into a stick puppet.

Here, There and Everywhere

Display a map of the United States. Show the children the state in which they live. Point out Washington state and Washington, D.C., which are both named after the famous President. Do they live near to or far from each? Next, share a picture of the Washington Monument, which is located in Washington, D.C., and was built to honor our first President. Compare the height of the monument to any surrounding trees or buildings in the picture. Has anyone in the class ever visited the monument?

Have the children make their own replicas of the monument from thin cardboard. Empty cereal boxes work well. Provide them with a pattern to trace and cut from the cardboard; then have them cover their monuments with aluminum foil.

Washington Coins

Share quarters with the children. Notice the size, color and shape of the coin. Name the pictures and/or numbers on both sides. Read the words on both sides to the class. Does anyone know how many cents a quarter is worth? Place a piece of rolled tape on several quarters and stick them to a sheet of paper. Be sure to show both sides of the quarter. Have the children place a sheet of paper over the taped coins, hold the paper in place and rub over the quarters with the side of a crayon to make coin prints.

The Real Thing

Share some real cherries with the class. Try to obtain some with leaves and stems intact. Talk about where cherries come from and name the parts (leaves, stems, fruit). Slice one open. Talk about what you find inside. Slice several more open. Allow the children to taste the fruit and have them plant the seeds to see if they can grow trees.

Cherry Letters

English muffins   sliced cherries   cream cheese

Slice and toast the English muffins. Spread cream cheese over the muffins. Place sliced cherries into the cream cheese in the shape of a W.

by Marie E. Cecchini

Holidays & Seasonal Celebrations, Issue 8, Teaching & Learning Co. © 1997, Carthage, IL 62321

Washington

Cherry Tree Legend

Discuss the following legend of George Washington and the cherry tree. As a boy, George receives a new hatchet which he tries out on one of his father's cherry trees. When his father questions the felled tree, George tells the truth and is not punished. Have the children share their thoughts on the story. Next, provide them with paper, brown markers, cotton swabs, red and green paint. Ask them to draw a tree trunk and branches on the paper with the brown marker. Then have them add cherries and leaves with the paints and cotton swabs.

Cherry Magnet

Have the children trace and cut out a small circle from thin cardboard. Color it brown. Cut brown pipe cleaners into 3" lengths. Have each child count out two pipe cleaner pieces; then glue one end of each piece to the cardboard circle. Have them glue a red pom-pom to the opposite end of each pipe cleaner piece. Provide them with green paper, markers and scissors to draw and cut out three leaves. Let them glue their leaves to the brown cardboard. Allow to dry. Then glue a magnet strip to the back of the cardboard.

Note: Do gluing on waxed paper. This makes the project easier to move for drying, and the waxed paper will peel easily off of any excess glue.

George Washington

When George Washington was a little kid,
(Show size of a small child.)

He was just like you and me.
(Point to others and self.)

One of the naughty things he did
(Put up index finger for "one.")

Was cut down a cherry tree!
(Pretend to swing an axe.)

His dad was mad and made George cry,
(Rub eyes.)

And George was very sad.
(Show a sad face.)

Then he said, "I cannot lie."
(Look up–serious and brave look.)

And both of them were glad.
(Smile broadly.)

by Judy Wolfman

Washington Bills

Share single dollar bills with the children. Who is on the front? Can they see his tiny name? Note the pictures on the back. Read the large word "one" and have the children name the letters. Count how many times the word appears on the front and back of the bill. Count how many numeral 1's are on the front and back of the bill. Explore the relationship between quarters and dollars.

CHINESE NEW YEAR

Chinese New Year is among the many holidays and customs of the Orient—it is probably the best known. At midnight on the 20th of February, the new year begins. This joyful and ceremonious holiday is celebrated with lion and dragon dances, fireworks, parades and eating special foods. The most common customs for families during this happy season are cleaning house, paying off debts, showing respect to older family members, giving and receiving money and sharing food with visitors.

Cleaning house is required to get rid of all bad fortune of the past, and it must be done during the last few days of the old year. Paying off old debts allows one to start the new year with a "clean slate." Food is important symbolically. Eating pink cake and red fruits means you will have good luck. Fish and pork symbolize a good harvest and that all wishes will come true. Excitement is in the air. Everyone wears new and colorful clothing to visit family members. It is customary for the children to receive money tucked away in red envelopes!

The worship of Buddha is part of the Chinese religion. It is said that he promised gifts to all the animals who came to pay him homage. Twelve animals came in the following order: rat, ox, tiger, rabbit, dragon, snake, horse, ram, monkey, cock, dog and boar. A year was named after each one. This makes up the 12-year Chinese zodiac. Each animal is used to identify a new year. The year is believed to have the characteristics of the animal it represents. Many believe that people born in a certain year will have some of the same characteristics of that animal and that the year will also determine what their life will be like!

Firsthand Experiences

If you know adults of Chinese background, perhaps one or several would be willing to be a guest speaker for the class. A field trip might be arranged to a local Chinese restaurant, where students could go "behind the scenes" and watch the preparation of different foods. Several Oriental cooking shows on television might be viewed.

Folk Wisdom

Philosophy can provide students with deep insights and understanding regarding different cultures through literature, the arts and the particular beliefs of that group. Read and discuss each of the following Chinese proverbs with students:

A lean dog shames his master.

Even a bad coin has two sides.

Done leisurely, done well.

After discussion, students can illustrate the proverbs. A class book might be started, adding sayings, stories and proverbs students find from other cultural groups.

by Teddy Meister

Chinese Zodiac

Year	Animal	Personality
1986	tiger	rebellious
1987	rabbit	happy
1988	dragon	lucky
1989	snake	wise
1990	horse	popular
1991	ram	charming
1992	monkey	mischievous
1993	rooster	aggressive
1994	dog	worried
1995	pig	gallant
1996	rat	nervous
1997	ox	patient

The cycle is repeated every 12 years.

Action Collage

Provide magazines and newspapers for cutting. Divide the class into 12 small groups. Assign each group an animal from the Chinese zodiac list and tell them to cut out pictures of that animal. Mount these on a large sheet of art paper, adding the year each represents. Display these as a colorful bulletin board collage.

Every Twelve Years

Make a copy of the Chinese zodiac chart for each student, or prepare one on a large chart for class use. The 12-year cycle starts with the rat. Have students identify which animal represents the current year. Next year? The year 2000? Can they determine the animal for the year they were born? The year they first started school?

Red Means "Good Luck!"

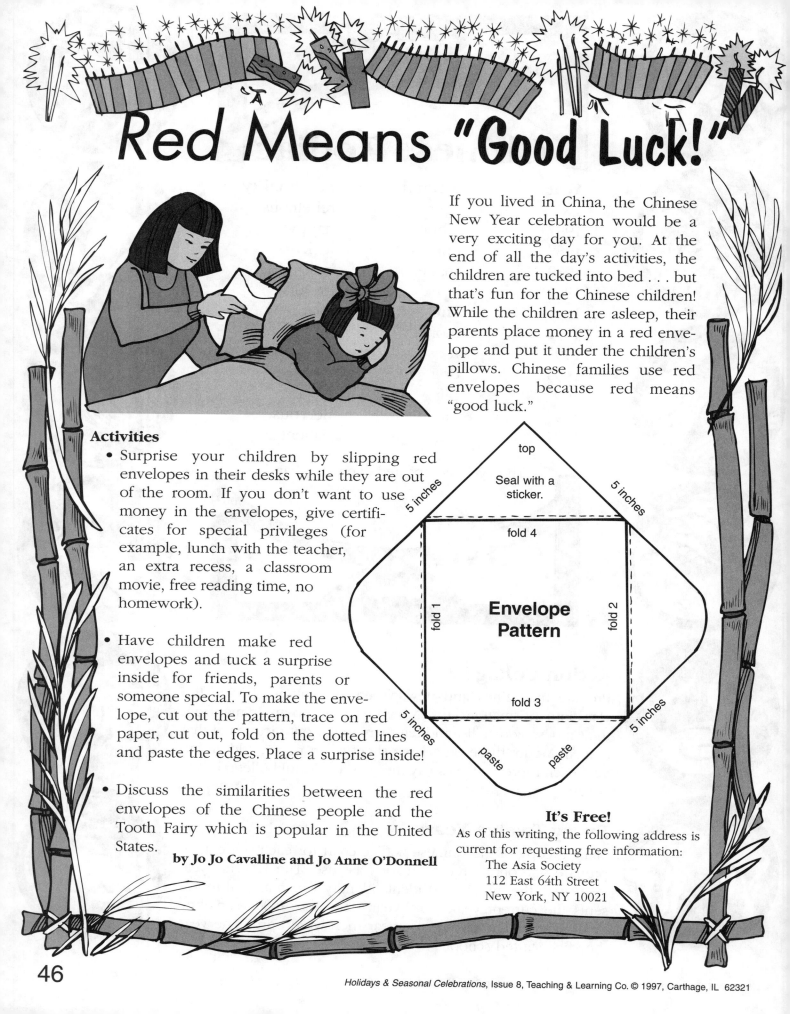

If you lived in China, the Chinese New Year celebration would be a very exciting day for you. At the end of all the day's activities, the children are tucked into bed . . . but that's fun for the Chinese children! While the children are asleep, their parents place money in a red envelope and put it under the children's pillows. Chinese families use red envelopes because red means "good luck."

Activities

• Surprise your children by slipping red envelopes in their desks while they are out of the room. If you don't want to use money in the envelopes, give certificates for special privileges (for example, lunch with the teacher, an extra recess, a classroom movie, free reading time, no homework).

• Have children make red envelopes and tuck a surprise inside for friends, parents or someone special. To make the envelope, cut out the pattern, trace on red paper, cut out, fold on the dotted lines and paste the edges. Place a surprise inside!

• Discuss the similarities between the red envelopes of the Chinese people and the Tooth Fairy which is popular in the United States.

by Jo Jo Cavalline and Jo Anne O'Donnell

top

Seal with a sticker.

5 inches   5 inches

fold 4

fold 1   **Envelope Pattern**   fold 2

fold 3

5 inches   5 inches

paste   paste

It's Free!

As of this writing, the following address is current for requesting free information:
The Asia Society
112 East 64th Street
New York, NY 10021

Holidays & Seasonal Celebrations, Issue 8, Teaching & Learning Co. © 1997, Carthage, IL 62321

St. Patrick's Day

Kid Space is a place of school yard beginnings. It is an ever-changing, fascinating place where children can connect with the natural world and learn all kinds of things. Kid Space is a safe place where kids can explore freely, embark on adventures, and make learning discoveries all on their own. Make the most of the smells, the colors, the textures, the sounds, the excitement, the freedom and the peace and quiet.

Ireland is famous for its lush green rolling hills. What better place to celebrate this holiday than out in the greenery!

Jig on the Green

The lively Irish Jig is a traditional dance of Ireland. Have children follow these easy instructions for some hop and jig fun. This activity is great for concentration, coordination and endurance. It might take a little practice, and not everyone will catch on, so allow a little creative license for children to hop and point and stamp to their own drummer! Take the hopping and jigging out to the green for some active, outdoor St. Patrick's Day fun.

1. Stand straight and proud with your feet placed together.

2. Put your hands on your hips—or for added effect, place the backs of your hands on your hips with your palms facing outward.

3. Put your left foot slightly forward and to the side and tap your heel on the ground once while you hop once on the right foot.

4. Hop once again on the right foot, but this time bend your left knee and point your left foot so the toes tap the ground in front of the right foot.

5. Hop for a third time on the right foot and bring the left foot back to the side with heel down on the ground.

6. Hop on the right foot for a fourth time and land with a bit of a stomp with both feet back together again.

7. Repeat the hopping-heel-toe process again, hopping on the left and then the right and so on.

• Add to the fun by bringing a portable music player out to the green with some lively Irish tunes.

Gold in the Greenery

There's nothing quite like a hunt for gold on St. Patrick's Day and no better place for it than in the greenery!

Hide shiny pennies, gold foil-wrapped pennies or gold-wrapped chocolate coins in a designated area of the school yard. Have students drop the coins they find in the "pot." Make this a cooperative exercise by asking students to find 100 coins in five minutes. Hide more coins than you ask the children to find. Have students drop the coins in the pot as they find them. The pot of gold can be used as manipulatives for math exercises and then shared by all.

Leprechaun's View

Have students get down to the leprechaun's level. How does nature look from down there? Do children notice anything they had not seen from their vantage point?

by Robynne Eagan

Learn *and* Play

Game for a Game?

Are you looking for exciting games to play anywhere, anytime, with little or no equipment or preparations? *Game for a Game?* shares the special secrets, folklore, lingo, hand signs, rhymes and rules of all sorts of games from the school yard to the street, from the playroom to the classroom. With some kids, chalk , a jump rope, jacks, a ball and a bag of rubber bands, the fun in this book is yours!

TLC10024 K-4 144 pp. $13.95

Indoor Games That Teach

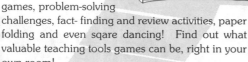

Motivate young learners, bring subjects to life and keep children active–even indoors! Children can master the basics (and more) by engaging their skills in board games, problem-solving challenges, fact- finding and review activities, paper folding and even sqare dancing! Find out what valuable teaching tools games can be, right in your own room!

TLC10068 K-4 144 pp. $13.95

Save on shipping and handling!

Contact your local school supply store! (See pages 78 and 79 for a store near you.) If you do not have a local school supply store, see page 80 or order toll free

1-800-852-1234

Teaching & Learning Company
1204 Buchanan St., P.O. Box 10, Carthage, IL 62321
1-800-852-1234 or 1-217-357-2591
Fax: 1-217-357-6789
e-mail: tandlcom@adams.net

Search for the Four-Leaf Clover

Host a hunt for a four-leaf clover. Encourage children to talk about the sights, smells, sounds and textures as they hunt through the foliage. The shamrock is a clover leaf—or trefoil—made up of three parts. The shamrock was considered a sacred plant by the early Irish settlers called the *Celts.* The four-leaf clover—which is very difficult to find—is thought to bring luck to those who find it.

Make a Lucky Charm
If you are lucky enough to find a four-leaf clover or can piece one together, you can make your very own Irish lucky charm.

You Need:
- four-leaf clover or reasonable facsimile
- two sheets of plain white paper
- flower press or heavy book
- white tagboard or construction paper
- clear adhesive plastic sheet
- scissors
- glue
- tweezers
- small paintbrush
- single hole punch
- green yarn

What to Do:
1. Place the four-leaf clover or two three-leaf clovers between the sheets of white paper. Place the white paper in a flower press or between the pages of a large, heavy book. Leave the clover to dry and press for three to four days.
2. Cut a circle from the white tagboard, large enough to frame your clover with a border edge.
3. Cut the clear adhesive plastic piece to extend about $1/8"$ around the edges of the tagboard.
4. Carefully paint glue on the back of the clover and place the four-leaf clover, or arrange the three-leaf with an extra petal, on the tagboard. Allow the arrangement to dry thoroughly before continuing.
5. With adult assistance, remove the backing from the plastic covering and carefully place over the tagboard and clover.
6. Cover the back of the tagboard with the second piece of covering.
7. Trim the edges to make them straight, and punch a hole in the top of the tagboard.
8. Thread green yarn through the hole so you can wear your lucky charm as a necklace or hang it as an ornament.

Did you know that clover is a sign of a healthy school yard? Clover fixes nitrogen in the soil, attracts beneficial insects and makes lawns appear very green.

Irish Green

When March winds welcome St. Patrick's Day, invite your students to experiment and create with the color green.

The Sharing of Green

Declare one day as Green Day. Ask that each child wear something green and bring in a green item from home to share at circle time. As the group discusses their green contributions, note the varying shades of green. Have the children suggest ways in which they think these different greens are made.

Sorting Shamrocks

Cover three coffee cans with white paper. Glue a different-sized green shamrock to the outside of each can (small, medium and large). Provide the students with several green poster board shamrocks of each size. Have them sort the shamrocks and drop them into the appropriate containers. Help them count how many they found of each size. Which group(s) has more, less or the same number of shamrocks?

Experimenting with Green

1. *Water Moves:* Pour a small amount of water into a clear plastic cup. Add a drop or two of green food coloring. Cut a strip from a coffee filter and place one end into the water. Observe the green water as it "crawls" up the white filter paper.

2. *The "Un"-Making of Green:* Pour a small amount of water into a clear plastic cup. Cut a second strip from the coffee filter. Color a narrow band of green, with washable marker across the strip, about one or two inches from the bottom. Place one end of the strip in the water. Observe the water as it climbs the paper strip and moves into the marker band. Continue to watch as the water separates the green. Help the children note the yellow and blue coloring as it appears.

by Marie E. Cecchini

Green Wall Hanging

Provide each child with glue and a strip of green paper about four inches wide. Poke two holes at the top of the paper and thread with green yarn for hanging. Supply a variety of green items, such as buttons, leaves, fabric scraps, pipe cleaners, beads, jug lids, yarn and sequins. Have them each create a green collage.

Green Sweep

Place two cardboard boxes on their sides, several feet away from the children. Two at a time, have the children use housekeeping brooms to sweep a green balloon across the floor and into one of the boxes.

Shamrock Places

Prepare one large and several small green felt shamrocks. Place the large shamrock on the flannel board. Ask individual children to select a small shamrock and give them specific directions for its placement on the flannel board. Suggestions: far from, next to (near), above, below, left, right, behind, in front of and so on.

Painting with Water

For this experiment, you will need three clear measuring cups, yellow and blue food coloring, a stirring spoon, water, white paper and cotton swabs. Fill two measuring cups with water. Add a few drops of yellow food coloring to one, and add blue to the other. Stir to mix in the color. Have the children observe as you pour part of each color of water into the empty measuring cup. What happens when the colors mix? Let the children use cotton swabs dipped into these watercolors to create pastel pictures on white paper.

Count and Search

Prepare a few paper shamrocks with varying numbers of dots. Place the shamrocks in a bag. Ask individual children to pull a shamrock out of the bag, count the dots, then search the room and point out the same number of green items. Place the shamrock back in the bag and give the bag a shake before the next person's turn. Encourage the children to choose green objects that have not already been "found."

50

Dancing Belts

Have each child cut out two green shamrocks. Help them trace the edges of each shamrock with white glue; then sprinkle gold glitter over the glue. Allow the glue to dry. Next, provide each child with a length of ribbon, heavy yarn or a fabric strip. Help them staple a shamrock to each end of their ribbons and tie these ribbon belts around their waists. Now gather the group into a circle and ask them to place their hands on their hips. Play some Irish dancing music and have them do a jump-kick dance. You may also want to try a "pattern dance" such as three jumps, two kicks.

Slimey Limey

For a manipulative material with a texture all its own, try this.

> 1 T. white glue
> 1 T. water
> green food coloring
> 2-3 tsp. Borax™ mixture*

*Borax™ mixture:
> 1 T. Borax™
> 1 c. warm water

Mix the white glue thoroughly with the water. Add a few drops of food coloring. Dissolve Borax™ in warm water. While stirring the glue mixture, slowly add two to three teaspoons of the Borax™ mixture until a ball is formed. Store in a plastic sandwich bag. **Note:** 1 T. glue and 1 T. water make enough for about two children.

Try stretching the green ball quickly, then slowly. Try bouncing it. Try holding one end of it up and see how it stretches.

Name Necklaces

Provide small pre-cut shamrocks for the children. Have them count out as many shamrocks as there are letters in their names. Help them write each letter on a separate shamrock with white glue; then sprinkle green glitter over the glue. When the letters are dry, provide children with green yarn and large blunt needles. Show them how to string their shamrocks from side to side to spell their names. As they complete their necklaces, tie the yarn ends to secure.

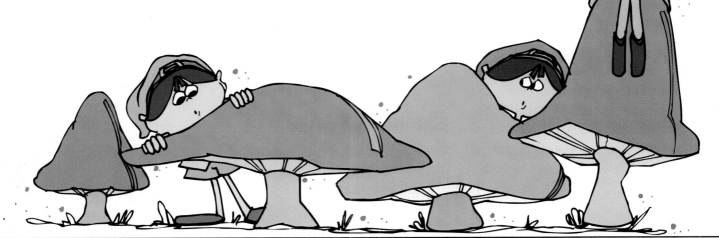

Green Is My Garden

Make individual planting trays by cutting several green Styrofoam™ egg cartons into two half-dozen sections. Provide the children with their own planting trays and allow them to place soil in each section. Supply seeds to grow "green things." You may want to refer to the fruit and vegetables from the "Green Food" tasting. Make a small sign for each garden, to label whose it is and what was planted. Tape the sign to a toothpick and insert it into one of the cups.

Sprinkle Paint

Fill old saltshakers and spice bottles with blue and yellow tempera paint. Provide the children with these paint shakers, white paper and spray bottles filled with water. Have the children sprinkle both paint colors onto the white paper. Then spray the papers with water. Note any color mixing.

Shamrock Flag

Let the children use a green marker to trace a large shamrock pattern on a 9" x 12" sheet of white paper. Have them sponge paint the shamrocks green. When dry, tape each flag to a cardboard paper towel tube.

Shamrock Shakers

Help the children use tape and green tissue paper to cover a bath tissue tube. Let them cut two circles from a brown paper bag. Secure one circle over an end of the tube with a rubber band. Have the children count out four or five dried peas and drop them into the open end of the tube. Secure the second circle over the open end with a rubber band. Provide shamrock stickers for the children to use to decorate their shakers.

Now put on some St. Patrick's Day music and have a parade with your flags and shakers.

Shamrock Puzzle

Supply the children with green paper, markers, scissors, a heart-shaped pattern and a triangle-shaped pattern. Have them each trace and cut out three hearts and one triangle. Display a picture of a shamrock and have the children fit their puzzle pieces together to form their own shamrocks. Provide them with envelopes for their pieces.

Shamrock Puzzle Math

Prepare several cards with a green triangle shape. On each triangle, write a different numeral. Prepare several heart shapes with a varying number of dots. Help the children select the correct hearts, by counting the dots, to place with each triangle so the numeral will equal the number of dots.

Green Food

Ask parents to contribute to a sampling session of green foods. Possibilities include: fruits, vegetables, jelly, juice, gelatin, ice cream and pudding. Help the children with naming any foods unfamiliar to them. Let them sample what they choose. Note if the green fruits and vegetables are also green on the inside.

Dish Garden

Cut shamrock shapes from green sponges. Have the children moisten the sponges and set them in plastic lids. Provide them with grass seed to sprinkle on top. Keep the sponges moist and observe as the grass grows.

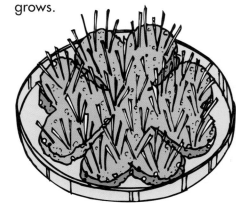

MISSING
The Lost Easter Bonnet

Help! Tansy Turtle has lost her new Easter bonnet, and she can't seem to find it anywhere! Grab your crayons and finish the "Missing" poster, using these instructions:

1. Color the bonnet yellow.
2. Draw 2 big orange and 3 small pink flowers on the bonnet.
3. Draw 4 green leaves on the flowers.
4. Draw a blue butterfly on the bonnet and color the bow red.
5. Add any other items to Tansy's bonnet that you wish.

Bonus: Write a story telling how Tansy's animal friends help find her missing bonnet.

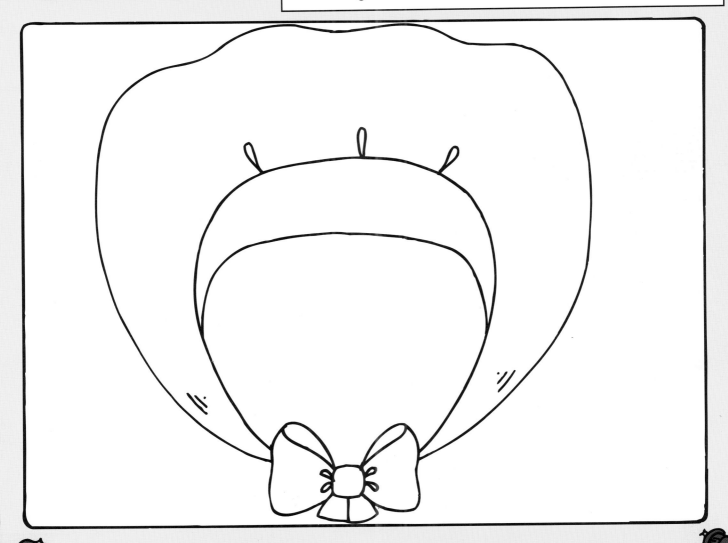

by Mary Ellen Switzer

Holidays & Seasonal Celebrations, Issue 8, Teaching & Learning Co. © 1997, Carthage, IL 62321

No Eggs

by Phyllis Brubaker Pyle

"I'm not going to color any eggs this year," Bunny announced one early spring day.

The hens in Bantam Henhouse stood up in their nests and opened their beaks in astonishment.

"Last year I sat in the pot of blue dye," complained Bunny. "I spilled red dye on my foot and accidentally colored my whiskers green. Then I got my nose too close to an egg I had just painted yellow. Painting eggs is just too much trouble."

"But it wouldn't be Easter without colorful eggs," objected Hattie Hen.

"What will you put in the baskets?" asked Harriet Hen.

Happy Hen was too astonished to say anything.

"I'll fill them with candy eggs," explained Bunny. "I won't have to worry about breaking *them.*"

"No real eggs for Easter!" exclaimed Hattie Hen.

"The children will be disappointed!" sighed Harriet Hen.

"Their parents will be upset!" cackled Happy Hen, even though she was still astonished.

"Oh, no," said Bunny. "The parents will be glad. Candy wrappers don't make a mess like eggshells. Now I must be going. Easter is just two days away, and I have lists to make." With these words, Bunny went hopping away to the room behind the henhouse where he had his workshop.

"We can't let Bunny ruin Easter this year!" exclaimed Hattie Hen.

"We've got to do something!" sighed Harriet Hen.

Holidays & Seasonal Celebrations, Issue 8, Teaching & Learning Co. © 1997, Carthage, IL 62321

"We'll put our beaks together and think of a plan," cackled Happy Hen. She did not sound very happy.

The hens hopped down from their nests. They gathered in a circle and tilted their heads this way and that as they thought and thought.

Soon Hattie Hen began to cackle. Harriet Hen cackled louder. Happy Hen got very excited and cackled loudest of all.

After Bunny had gone home to bed, the hens marched into his workshop.

Hattie Hen moved the eggs by rolling them with her beak.

Harriet Hen mixed the dyes together.

Happy Hen used the tips of her wing feathers to splash the colors on the eggs. Sometimes she splashed the eggs. Sometimes she splashed herself and Hattie and Harriet Hen.

Bunny came to the workshop the next morning. "What have you done?" he cried when he saw the spots of gold, brown, red and blue dye all over everything.

"We couldn't let you ruin Easter!" exclaimed Hattie Hen.

"We colored the eggs for you!" sighed Harriet Hen.

"I'm afraid we colored ourselves, too," cackled Happy Hen.

Bunny looked at the baskets of colored eggs. "These are the most beautiful eggs I've ever seen," he said. "I can't wait to deliver them."

The three hens fluffed their many-colored feathers as they cackled happily.

And ever since that day, all Bantam hens in the henhouse have been speckled with many different colors.

Bunny Land

Invite your children to hop on over to "Bunny Land" for some fun-filled Easter activities.

Bunny Breakfast

Begin your day the healthy way by creating a delicious "bunny" dish.

What You Need:
English muffins
soft cream cheese
sliced melon
strawberries
red grapes
blueberries
raisins

What to Do:
Toast the muffins. Spread cream cheese on a muffin half and set it on a plate. Cut a melon slice in half and place the halves above the muffin head for ears. Slice a red grape in half and press the halves into the cream cheese for eyes. Slice a strawberry in half and place one half below the eyes for a nose. Position rows of raisins on either side of the nose for whiskers. Give your bunny a smiling, blueberry mouth.

A Bunny Tail

Draw a rearview picture of a rabbit on a cardboard box. Draw a circle to mark the tail position. Glue several strips of Velcro™ inside the circle. Provide the children with sock balls or foam balls. Have them take turns tossing the balls at the box. When a ball sticks to the Velcro™, the bunny will have its tail. (gross motor skills)

Bunny Bracelet

Cut several 1" circular strips from a cardboard tube. Slice each strip so it will open. Provide the children with white paper, scissors, markers and a small bunny pattern. Have them trace, color and cut out their bunnies. Staple each bunny to a cardboard strip. Open the strip and slide it onto the child's wrist.   (scissor skills)

Box Garden

Make use of shoe box lids, green paper and garden catalogs to "plant" a garden fit for a rabbit. Cut the green paper into strips. Have the children use scissors to fringe the strips for grass. Glue this grass around the edges of the lid, forming a framed, rectangular garden area. Let the children cut fruit and vegetable pictures from the garden catalogs to plant in their gardens with glue. (scissor skills)

Note: Bunny patterns for the various activities on these pages are located on page 74.

by Marie E. Cecchini

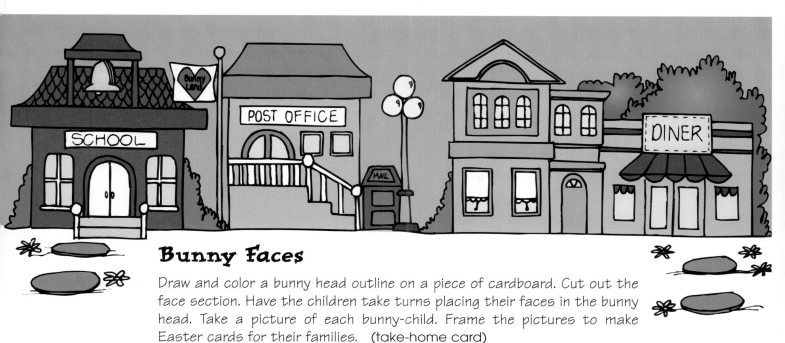

Bunny Faces

Draw and color a bunny head outline on a piece of cardboard. Cut out the face section. Have the children take turns placing their faces in the bunny head. Take a picture of each bunny-child. Frame the pictures to make Easter cards for their families.   (take-home card)

Bunny Math

Ask the children to bring in stuffed bunny toys from home. Have them introduce their bunnies to the class.

Bunny Sorting: Provide color-coded boxes or baskets for the children to use in sorting the stuffed animals by color. Tabulate the sorting results on a color graph. For each bunny in each color basket, place one rabbit sticker in the correct graph column. What color are most of the bunnies? Which color has the least number of bunnies?

Bunny Sizes: 1. Make use of several different-sized bunnies. Have the children arrange these from largest to smallest, mix them all together again, then arrange them from smallest to largest.
2. Separate the stuffed rabbits into three piles: small, medium and large. Count to see which group has the most/least rabbits. Do any groups have the same number of rabbits?

Bunny Count: Carefully count the whole bunny collection. Write the number on a sheet of paper. Where else can we find this same number? Can you find it on the clock or on the calendar?

Baby Bunny Baskets

Baskets: Punch a hole in both sides of a one-pound margarine tub. Fasten the ends of a pipe cleaner through the holes to make a handle. Let the children decorate the containers with Easter stickers. Place Easter grass in each basket.

Baby Bunny: Glue two cotton balls together, one on top of the other, to form a bunny head and body. Glue two small pink ears to the back of the head. Add two black hole-punch eyes, a pink triangle nose, yarn-snip whiskers and a yarn snip mouth. Place the baby bunny in its basket to dry.   (small motor skills, following directions)

Bunny Trail Tricks

Have the children pretend to be bunnies delivering eggs as they move through a bunny trail obstacle course. You might have them jump over a block, crawl under a table, walk a wavy length of yarn on the floor, shimmy through a cardboard box and walk in and out through a row of chairs. Let them each carry one small, plastic egg to be deposited in a basket at the end of the trail.   (gross motor skills)

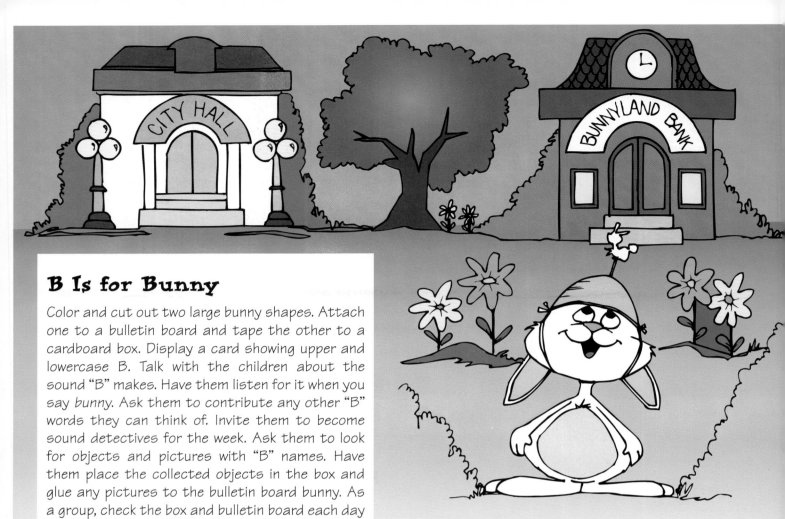

B Is for Bunny

Color and cut out two large bunny shapes. Attach one to a bulletin board and tape the other to a cardboard box. Display a card showing upper and lowercase B. Talk with the children about the sound "B" makes. Have them listen for it when you say bunny. Ask them to contribute any other "B" words they can think of. Invite them to become sound detectives for the week. Ask them to look for objects and pictures with "B" names. Have them place the collected objects in the box and glue any pictures to the bulletin board bunny. As a group, check the box and bulletin board each day for any new additions.

Bunny in a Hole

Cut oatmeal or salt boxes in half. Cover the cylinder with green paper, poke a hole in the bottom and fill with Easter grass. Have each child cut out a small bunny from pink or white paper and color it. Tape the bunny to the top of a drinking straw or craft stick. Slide the opposite end of the straw or stick through the hole under the grass. The children can then hold the box in one hand and move the straw or stick with the other hand to make the bunny hop into and up from the grass.

the bowl, thread with elastic cord and tie to fit under each child's chin. Have the children color and cut out their own bunnies. Tape each bunny to the top of a pipe cleaner. Poke the opposite end of the pipe cleaner through the hat and tape it to the inside. The bunnies will wiggle and hop when the children wear their beenies.

Bunny Cup

Make cute Bunny Cups for storing tiny treasures or colorful jelly beans. Supply the children with Styrofoam™ cups, pink paper, pink pom-poms, black pipe cleaners, scissors, glue and markers. Have them draw eyes on the cup and cut out two pink ears to glue at the top. Let them glue on a pom-pom nose and cut out a pink mouth to glue at the bottom. When the glue is dry, poke both ends of a pipe cleaner from the inside of the cup to the outside on either side of the nose for whiskers. Bend to shape. Add a second pipe cleaner in the same manner.

Holidays & Seasonal Celebrations, Issue 8, Teaching & Learning Co. © 1997, Carthage, IL 62321

What Rabbits Do
(to the tune of "Frere Jacques")
I'm a rabbit. I'm a rabbit.
See what I do. See what I do.
Here at school, here at school.
I can munch a carrot.
I can munch a carrot.
Here at school.
Here at school.

(Variations: hop on one foot, hop on two feet, wrinkle my nose, bend my ears, wiggle my tail)

Snack Hop

Place a container of carrot sticks on a chair a few feet from the children. Mark a starting line. Have individual children begin at the starting line and hop to the carrots, counting how many hops each takes to receive a carrot. Remind them to sit while they munch their carrots. Bunnies cannot hop and eat at the same time.

Bunny Parade

Invite the children to use doll clothes and dress their bunnies for a parade. Help with any buttons, snaps or zippers as necessary. Play music as they march around with their animals. Have them line up the animals single file and clap to the music while the animals have their own parade.

Bunny Habits

Let the children take turns leading the group in imitating rabbit actions to the song above.

Bunny Bags

Draw several rabbit faces. Staple each to the top front of a paper lunch bag. Write a different number on each bag. Fasten the back of each bag to a bulletin board. Provide the children with a container of orange manipulatives such as marker lids, jug lids or beads. These are the pretend carrots. Have individual children read the numbers on the bags; then feed the bunnies the correct number of carrots by dropping manipulatives in the bags.

in a Shopping Bag

An Easter Story

"I don't know what old people like," complained Matthew. "Besides, I don't see why we should have to spend our spring break working. Why can't we just have fun?"

"Because," said his mother, in the same pitiful tone of voice that Matthew had used with such skill, "it isn't just spring break. This is the week before Easter, a special time for us."

"Special like big chocolate rabbits and hunting for eggs in the park?" asked Matthew. He had perked up considerably.

"I imagine there will be some of that," smiled his mother. "But there will be something more."

"More treats!" exclaimed Matthew, doing a little dance.

"More *treating* other people," finished his mother.

"Like visiting the old folks' home," sighed Matthew. He had stopped dancing and started slumping over the basket that his mother had been packing.

"I found the bars of soap," a cheerful voice wafted into the room. Behind it came Mrs. Anderson and her daughter, Ashlynn. Matthew and Ashlynn were the same age, nine years old; and their families were close friends.

"Rose-scented and honeysuckle-scented soap will perk up our friends at the County Rest Home," smiled Mrs. Anderson. Matthew peeked into her bulging shopping bag; even he had to smile at the delightful scents!

Ashlynn added, "We found some of the softest wash-cloths to put in the basket, too. They'll feel nice on the older folks' delicate skin." Ashlynn had been to the County Rest Home before, and she knew how much the residents enjoyed the small gifts.

While the two moms packed their baskets and bags, Ashlynn and Matthew moved outside to load a dozen small pots of mums into the mini van. The mums made a bold, springtime rainbow on the van floor: lavender, yellow and peach-colored.

by Dr. Linda Karges-Bone

Holidays & Seasonal Celebrations, Issue 8, Teaching & Learning Co. © 1997, Carthage, IL 62321

"These flowers are going to brighten up the rooms," noted Ashlynn. "And they could use some color."

"Why don't they just buy some paint and pictures and stuff, like *we* do to decorate?" asked Matthew.

"It's not that simple, Matt," Ashlynn told her friend. "The folks in the County Rest Home don't have much money, or hardly anyone else to take care of them. Their monthly checks are just enough to pay for their beds and food."

"Is that why my mom and your mom and some of the people at the church go out there . . . to bring stuff that they can't buy? Is that why we're bringing all these bags and baskets?"

"That's it . . . partly," answered Ashlynn. "But it has to do with helping others because you want to, because it is the right way to live." Ashlynn emphasized her words, too, but they didn't sound quite the same as Matt's grumbling.

Matthew thought about this all the way to the County Rest Home.

He and Ashlynn pulled down a red wagon, and loaded it with the potted blooms of color. Pulling it into the cool, dark hall of the nursing home, Matt noticed how bright the colored mums looked against the pale walls and grey floor.

In the day room, Mrs. Anderson and Matt's mother greeted the nurse who was on duty. Ashlynn walked over to greet a lady who was sitting in a wheelchair. She hugged the lady and smiled.

"Little boy!" a quavering voice called.

Matt turned around. He saw an older gentleman, wearing a plaid shirt, khaki pants and a baseball cap.

"Did you bring any LIFE-SAVERS®?" asked the old man. Matt looked around for his mother, but she was busy unwrapping a bunny cake that had an ear problem. *Somebody* had jabbed

at the icing with his finger, stealing a taste, and the ear had lost its hold on the bunny cake.

Guiltily, Matt turned around. "LIFESAVERS®? Do you mean me?"

"The colored ones, different colors in a roll. I can't get those kind here."

Matthew remembered the brown shopping bag left in the mini van. "Hold on a second," he yelled and ran outside.

Dragging the bag back to the day room, Matt plucked out a shiny new roll of candy. "Here you go."

"Darn these fingers," fussed the old man. "Arthritis has got 'em bad. Can't do a thing." He fumbled with the paper wrapping.

"I'll do it," Matthew offered. He unwrapped the candy and handed it to the old man. A red disk was first in the roll.

"Don't care for the red ones. You take it, boy," urged the old man.

"Okay." Matt popped the red one into his mouth."

"I'll take that yellow one," piped in a lady wearing a flowered robe and pink slippers. Matt carried it over to her, since she was leaning on a metal walker.

"Now, the green one. My favorite," declared the old man. He placed the green candy in his mouth and smiled. Matthew smiled, too.

"How come you can't get LIFESAVERS®?" he asked his new friend.

"Nowhere to go for them and no money to buy 'em if I could get away," he replied. "You get tired of not having your own things around you or being able to go when you want to."

"I like to get on my bike and ride to the store," agreed Matthew. He was beginning to understand.

The old man (his name was Mr. Ruppert Dawson) began telling Matthew about a bicycle that he had ridden 50 years earlier. "During the war, that would be World War II, gas was rationed, so I rode my bicycle to town when we needed something."

The old lady in the walker, Miss Helena, scooted over and told about her bicycle that once had a large wicker basket on the back. She had ridden the bicycle, using the basket to hold her books, to get to her teaching job in a one-room schoolhouse. That happened 60 years earlier. Miss Helena, he found out, was 82 years old.

Matthew, Mr. Ruppert Dawson and Miss Helena talked about bicycles and finished off a whole roll of LIFESAVERS® before they heard some lively music coming from across the day room. Ashlynn was playing "Camptown Races" on the piano. All around the day room, people were nodding and smiling. One lady, who wore dark, thick glasses, clapped her hands.

The smell of honeysuckle, a splash of rainbow-colored flowers and the sound of tinkling music had transformed the dark room. "It feels," thought Matthew, "like springtime has come inside." Something had changed, in the room *and* inside Matthew. "Just like the springtime changes the world around us. It's not just bringing beautiful baskets; it's *why* you bring the baskets that counts."

As they drove home from the County Rest Home, Matt reminded his mother, "Don't forget to get more LIFESAVERS® for our next visit and some raisins. Mr. Ruppert Dawson misses raisins in his oatmeal in the mornings."

From then on, LIFESAVERS® in a shopping bag, not chocolate in a basket, made Matthew think of Easter.

Holidays & Seasonal Celebrations, Issue 8, Teaching & Learning Co. © 1997, Carthage, IL 62321

Teaching Across the Curriculum with "LIFESAVERS®"

Language Arts

1. **Flavor Word Brainstorm:** Use a blank piece of chart paper and scented, colored markers to record the children's responses to the prompt: "How many flavors or flavor words can you think of?" Here are some to get you started: chocolate, raspberry, malt . . . .

2. **Sweet Adjectives:** Use the LIFESAVERS® candy pattern and provide three to six colored construction paper pieces of candy for each child. Use the disks to write adjectives that describe pleasant tastes. String the adjective candies into necklaces to wear or to adorn the room. Here are some examples of appropriate adjectives: sweet, tasty, delicious . . . .

3. In many ways, the "LIFESAVERS®" story is one of contrasts. This makes it a good choice for introducing or reinforcing antonyms, words that mean the opposite of each other. Create an Opposites Attract game by using the LIFESAVERS® candy pattern to make pairs of antonyms from the story, as well as others. Randomly select children and tape an antonym LIFESAVERS® to their backs. Let the children mix and mingle until they have found their "match." Each pair can be rewarded with real LIFESAVERS® candies. Examples: old-young, dark-light, sweet-sour, wrinkled-smooth.

Creative Arts Activities

1. **LIFESAVERS® Designs:** Use inexpensive rolls of colored disk candies, colored and plain toothpicks and white art paper to set up a center for designing creative pictures. The stark contrast between the jewel-like candies and the plain paper, and the simple addition of the toothpicks as connectors, gives the children many varied opportunities for design. Supply white glue to fasten the designs onto the paper.

2. **LIFESAVERS® Collages:** Use the LIFESAVERS® candy pattern to reproduce multicolored "candies" for the children to cut out and arrange in interesting patterns on butcher paper or freezer paper. Then select magazine or newspaper photographs of older and younger people and create a "people collage" on top of the existing LIFESAVERS® mosaic for a sort of "stained glass" effect. (Note: Use the magazine and newspaper pictures from the social studies activity. This is a logical enrichment or follow-up.)

Social Studies and Science

1. **Picture Perfect:** Prepare a file of photographs and pictures of both older and younger people. Display random pictures on a bulletin board, and engage the children in a discussion of how our lives and roles change with age. Here are some probing questions:

   - Is life easier or more difficult when one is older/younger? Why?

   - How do you treat older people? How *should* we treat older people?

   - Why should we respect older citizens? How can we show them that we respect and care about them?

   - What can younger people learn from older friends?

2. **Scents Alive:** Many of the incidents in the story contain descriptions of how we use our senses to interpret the world around us. Collect objects such as scented soap, a soft washcloth, raisins and others. Place these objects into a brown paper bag, and then invite individual children (blindfolded) to touch and smell the objects in the bag. How did they feel? Use the following observational checklist to complete the activity. Then place it in your science portfolios.

Mathematics and Problem Solving

1. LIFESAVERS® and raisins are easy and fun to use to introduce grouping concepts such as multiplication or division. Give each group of four children a paper cup of LIFESAVERS® or raisins and challenge them to solve the following problems. Small chalkboards are nice to use for recording the results. The group recorder can write the answer and hold up the board for instant checking.

   - Matthew and Ashlynn want to bring two friends each to help out on their next visit to the rest home. How many children can we count on?

   - The red wagon can hold seven plants. How many trips will Ashlynn and Matt have to make if they have 10 plants?

   - Matthew's mom included 15 bars of scented soap and 18 washcloths in her basket. How can you figure out how many extra washcloths she packed?

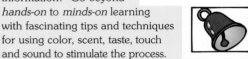

Holidays & Seasonal Celebrations, Issue 8, Teaching & Learning Co. © 1997, Carthage, IL 62321

Decorated Eggs

Students can decorate eggs using white glue and many common household products.

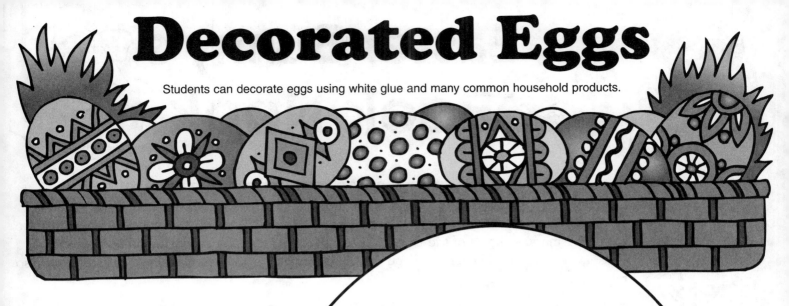

1. Cut out several of the egg shapes from cardboard using the pattern on the right. Students will use this to trace.

2. After students trace the egg shape on white paper, they can decorate it by drawing lines, circles, faces, zig-zags or other designs.

3. Apply white glue (the kind in a squeeze bottle works best) to one part of the design. Sprinkle one of the suggested items on the glue. Let that dry and shake off the excess. Apply glue to another section of the design and sprinkle another item on that section. Continue until the eggs are completely decorated.

4. Students can cut out the finished eggs after they dry and hang them from a tree or use them as classroom decorations.

Note: This project can be rather messy. You might want to spread newspaper over a large table and let students work together in one area rather than at individual desks.

Items to use for decorating eggs:

seashells

uncooked rice

colored sand or gravel

Cheerios™, Rice Krispies™ or other types of dry cereal

sunflower seeds or other small seeds

uncooked macaroni or other noodles

various colored dried beans

popped popcorn

colored sugar

peanuts

by Cindy Barden

Holidays & Seasonal Celebrations, Issue 8, Teaching & Learning Co. © 1997, Carthage, IL 62321

Easter Bunny's Book Nook

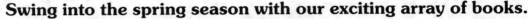

Swing into the spring season with our exciting array of books.

Peter Cotton Tail's Easter Book by Lulu Delacre (New York: Scholastic, Inc., 1991) is full of Eastertime surprises. Follow Peter Cottontail as he delivers his colorful eggs, and you can learn about the many symbols of the Easter season. Have fun singing an Easter version of "Itisket, Itasket," and try an old-fashioned egg roll. Directions for dyeing some sensational eggs are also included.

For Easter decorations galore, *175 Easy-to-Do Easter Crafts,* edited by Sharon Dunn Umnik (Boyds Mills Press, 1994), is the perfect book for you. Seasonal baskets, eggs, greeting cards and other holiday treasures will delight your class. Some of the crafts include Chick Finger puppet, Bunny Party Cups and Easter Place Mats. There are even directions for a felt board egg hunt game and a glitter egg mobile.

Winnie the Pooh's Easter

by Bruce Talkington; illustrated by Bill Langley and Diana Wakeman. New York: Disney Press, 1996.

Wow, what an egg! Winnie the Pooh and his friends gather around a giant-sized Easter egg that Pooh has found. When Rabbit tells them that an Easter egg can talk, Pooh and his friends try some plans to make the silent egg speak.

• Surprise! You find the *biggest* Easter egg in the world. Draw a picture of what the egg looks like. Tell what you would do with it.

• Do you know what bird lays the largest egg? It's the ostrich. Find out more about this amazing bird. Look in an encyclopedia or book about birds to help you. Create an *Amazing Ostrich* book with pictures and facts.

Happy Easter, Dear Dragon

by Margaret Hillert; illustrated by Carl Kock. Cleveland: Modern Curriculum Press, 1981.

Come along and join a boy and his pet dragon as they enjoy the Easter season. Making a necklace of spring flowers, decorating eggs and marching in an Easter parade are some of the highlights of their holiday.

• "D" is for dragon. Make a list of all the words in the story that begin with "d." Now put your list in alphabetical order.

• Happy birthday! You get a most unusual birthday gift this year—a pet dragon. Draw a picture of your new pet. Tell how you would take care of it.

• You decide to take your dragon to a neighborhood Easter egg hunt. It's a day you will never forget! Tell what happens.

by Mary Ellen Switzer

66

The Big Bunny and the Easter Eggs

by Steven Kroll; illustrated by Janet Stevens. New York: Scholastic, Inc., 1982.

Wilbur the Easter Bunny is all ready to deliver Easter baskets. The eggs are all painted, and there's lots of jelly beans and chocolate candy. Seems there's just one problem—Wilbur has a cold. Can he still deliver the Easter baskets?

- Poor Wilbur! It's time for him to deliver Easter baskets and he has a cold. Write a story telling how you came to his rescue.

- Help Wanted! Pretend that the Easter Bunny needs a new artist to paint eggs. Write an ad for this new job.

- Cartoon caper. Create a comic strip version of this story.

Bunny Trouble

by Hans Wilhelm. New York: Scholastic, Inc., 1985.

Easter is coming, and all the bunnies are hard at work decorating eggs for the big day. Everyone except Ralph is busy that is. All he wants to do is play soccer. Ralph soon finds himself in trouble when he practices his dribble in a farmer's cauliflower field.

- Happy Easter, Ralph! Design a special Easter egg for Ralph with a soccer theme.

- Calling all soccer fans! Create a brand-new game using a soccer ball. Write directions for playing your game.

- Think of a catchy name for your new game. Draw a billboard sign to advertise this amazing game.

The Great Big Especially Beautiful Easter Egg

by James Stevenson. New York: Greenwillow Books, 1983.

In this humorous Easter tale, a grandfather reminisces with his grandchildren about his journey many years ago to hunt for the world's greatest Easter egg. The children are in for an Easter surprise when they discover that the egg is still around after all these years.

- When he was younger, the grandfather traveled to the Frammistan Mountains in search of the world's greatest egg. Draw a picture of one event during his journey.

- You have all heard the old saying "An apple a day keeps the doctor away." Now finish this one: "An egg a day _____."

Easter Parade

by Mary Chalmers. HarperTrophy, 1988.

Join a lively group of animals as they gather to collect Easter baskets for a special parade. When there is one tiny basket left, the animals search everywhere to find the missing animal. Who can it be?

- Draw a picture of your favorite animal in the Easter parade. Write two sentences about the animal.

- Make a list of all the words you can think of using the letters in *Easter parade*.

- Plan an Easter parade that everyone would rave about. Draw a picture showing what your parade would look like.

Egg-a-Thon Book Week

The Easter season is a perfect time for an Egg-a-Thon Book Week. Delight your students with books and activities featuring an egg theme. Here are some "egg"cellent read-aloud favorites your class will enjoy:

Chickens Aren't the Only Ones by Ruth Heller. Grosset & Dunlap, 1981.

Egg Story by Anca Hariton. Dutton Children's Books, 1992.

Green Eggs and Ham by Dr. Seuss. Random House, 1960.

Horton Hatches the Egg by Dr. Seuss. Random House, 1940.

Rechenka's Eggs by Patricia Polacco. Philomel Books, 1988.

The Easter Egg Artists by Adrienne Adams. Charles Scribner's Sons, 1976.

The Easter Egg Farm by Mary Jane Auch. Holiday House, 1992.

The Golden Egg Book by Margaret Wise Brown. Golden Book, 1947.

The Most Wonderful Egg in the World by Helme Heine. Atheneum, 1983.

The Surprise Family by Lynn Reiser. Greenwillow Books, 1994.

Seasonal Borders

Use the months of January, February and March to make creative borders for holiday or seasonal bulletin boards. You'll teach the skills of cutting and following directions in the process.

Cut one 8 1/2" x 11" sheet of paper into three equal strips. Fold accordion-style as shown. Cutting one pattern makes four shapes. Make enough strips to outline a bulletin board for this holiday or season. Students may choose an appropriate color or decorate creatively.

January—snowman
February—tooth for Dental Health Month
February—heart for Valentine's Day
February—top hat for Lincoln's birthday or Presidents' Day
March—shamrock for St. Patrick's Day
March—bunny or duck for Easter

by Carolyn Tomlin

Tape pattern on top and cut around...

(Don't cut here!)   (Don't cut here!)

Decorate!

Holiday Classroom Decorations

Profiles of Great Americans

During the months of January and February, America honors three great men: Abraham Lincoln; George Washington and Dr. Martin Luther King, Jr. As you teach about these leaders, make a profile of each man and place on the bulletin board or in the hallway near your room. Also include profiles of students and place on the same bulletin board.

To make profiles, have each student sit on a stool with a large sheet of white paper attached to the wall behind him or her. Shine a large flashlight on the student. Quickly draw the outline with a black marker. The students copy this on black construction paper and then cut it out and paste on white paper.

by Carolyn Ross Tomlin

Heart Mobile

Here's a lovely way to decorate your classroom on Valentine's Day. Cut 1" strips of 12" x 18" red construction paper. Repeat this procedure using white and pink construction paper. Next, trim 2" from the top of the white strips and 4" off the top of the pink strips. Finally, cut out a 3" red heart for the center.

To begin assembly take one red strip, one white strip, one pink strip and a 3" red heart. Fold each strip in half and staple the bottom. Place all the top edges together and curve inward to form a heart. Staple all six strips together at once. You should have three colored hearts that are nested inside each other. Have the child write his or her name on the 3" heart, and then suspend it from the center of the nested strips. Hang these mobiles around your room for a lovely Valentine's decoration.

by Ann Scheiblin

Presidential Mobile

Hand out copies of a star shape. Pattern provided on page 72. As students use and gather information about Presidents, ask them to fill in the places on the stars with what they have found. Then decorate the star. These can be made into class mobiles. Use the points of the star to list some interesting events that took place when the President was in office.

by Teddy Meister

Paper Plate Easter Bunny

Simple materials help little hands become creative. Ordinary paper plates become an unusual Easter bunny.

Materials:
- 2 paper plates
- 3 chenille stems
- felt-tip markers
- scissors
- glue

Use one plate as the bunny's face. Cut the other plate into two ears and a bow tie. Draw eyes, mouth and nose. Cut small slits and insert the chenille stems. Staple the ears and bow tie on the head.

Use these bunnies as room decorations during the Easter and spring season. Or read a story about rabbits and use them as puppets.

by Carolyn Ross Tomlin

Holidays & Seasonal Celebrations, Issue 8, Teaching & Learning Co. © 1997, Carthage, IL 62321

Snowmen on Parade

Listen as your teacher reads these directions:

1. Draw a hat on the first snowman.
2. Give the second snowman a happy face.
3. Place a broom to the right of the third snow-man.

4. Draw a wig on the second snowman.
5. Draw a surprised look on the third snowman.
6. Make a funny face on the first snowman.
7. Give each snowman three buttons.
8. Draw a sun over the last snowman.

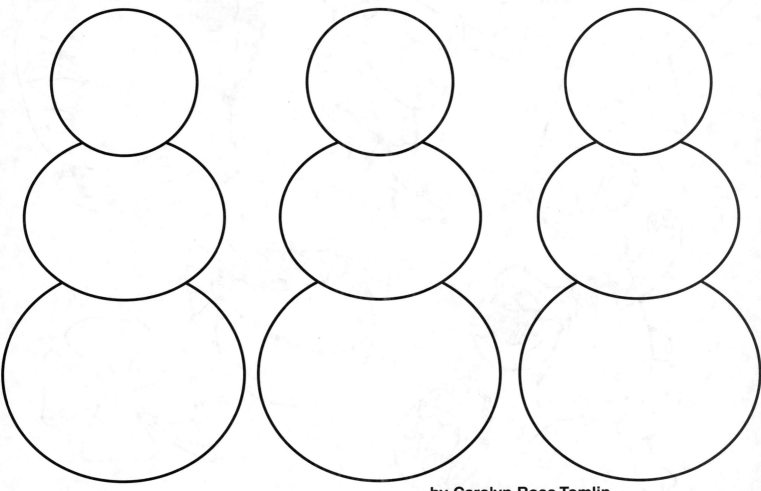

by Carolyn Ross Tomlin

Holidays & Seasonal Celebrations, Issue 8, Teaching & Learning Co. © 1997, Carthage, IL 62321

Teaching & Learning Company Poster Papers

Two-sided, black and white posters fold open to 22 1/4" x 17 1/4".
Each poster package retails for $9.95 and contains 30 posters.

PRIMARY

front   center   back
Amazing ME

TLC10038 Amazing ME preK-2
Lots of creative activities to encourage self-awareness in this circus-themed poster. Young children can make a thumbprint picture, draw and color pictures of their families and more!

TLC10048 My Body K-2
Children use their five senses, trace their feet, fill in their birth certificate and more using age-appropriate activities to make learning about the body lots of fun!

TLC10049 I Can Save the Earth K-2
Build environmental awareness with child-centered ideas and activities and suggest ways to protect the air, land, Earth and water.

TLC10036 Starring ME Gr. 2-6
The spotlight shines on information about each child, such as favorite things and family and friends, as they complete the Hollywood theme in this self-concept poster.

TLC10060 Electing a President Gr. 3 and up
Interactive fill-ins get students involved in the electoral process and can be used with fictional characters anytime or to track actual candidates in an election year.

TLC10061 My Favorite President Gr. 3 and up
Children can interview one of the 42 pictured Presidents or create one of their own as they collect important information about their favorite President.

TLC10062 My Favorite State Gr. 3 and up
Students select a state, then fill in fun facts and information about it such as: the capital, flag, motto, famous residents, historical events, local food and more.

TLC10063 My Favorite Country Gr. 4 and up
Children will discover fascinating facts about the history, people, geography and culture of the nation of their choice, as well as famous places and celebrated sights.

TLC10087 Dr. Martin Luther King, Jr. Gr. 3 and up
Open-ended format gets students involved with facts and information about this famous American leader.

INTERMEDIATE

front   center   back
Electing a President

Teaching & Learning Company . . .
What every child needs!

100 Best Ideas for Primary Language Arts

Poetry Party, Animal Alliteration, Punctuation Pals and Metaphor Madness are just a few of the 100 creative, skill-building ideas found in this comprehensive collection.

TLC10001   K-3   112 pp.   **$9.95**

100 Best Ideas for Primary Science

Students will become actively engaged in exploring the world around them as they discover how things work in our world, the science of living things, their bodies and the Earth.

TLC10002   K-3   112 pp.   **$9.95**

100 Best Ideas for Primary Math

Pegging Numbers, Celebrate 100, Feely Flash Cards, Number Museum and Shop 'Til You Drop! are just a few of the 100 exciting ideas compiled for this easy-to-use resource.

TLC10003   K-3   112 pp.   **$9.95**

Mother Goose and Friends

Each book is a comprehensive collection of craft projects, writing suggestions, circle time activities, games, cut-and-paste creations, action songs, plays and more! Reinforce the introduction of the ABCs and 123s with these two resources.

Each book is preK-3, 352 pages and **$24.95**.

TLC10000   *Mother Goose and Friends: An Alphabet Activity Book*

TLC10011   *Mother Goose and Friends: A Number Activity Book*

Teaching & Learning Company, 1204 Buchanan St., P.O. Box 10, Carthage, IL 62321
1-800-852-1234 or 1-217-357-2591   Fax: 1-217-357-6789   e-mail: tandlcom@adams.net
Save on shipping and handling! Contact your local school supply store! (See pages 78 and 79 for a store near you.)
If you do not have a local school supply store, see page 80 or order toll free 1-800-852-1234!

In-service workshops

are currently available . . .

Developmentally Appropriate Practices

Practical, classroom application of a developmental philosophy. Gain confidence in your knowledge of what is appropriate for young children's learning and be ready to take a look at your own developmental program.

Early Childhood Assessment Practices

A developmentally appropriate assessment program designed by the people who know the child the best, the teachers, to provide information to parents about their child.

Designing Early Childhood Learning Centers

Shows you how, why and when to use learning centers in your classroom. Learn to develop your own learning center curriculum or find a wealth of ideas to help you make your centers work more effectively.

Self-Esteem: What Every Student Needs

An experiential and informative seminar designed to help you enhance your students' self-esteem. Various fun-filled activities are presented which will give you a unique experience of professional and personal development.

Teaching & Learning Company consultants are available to conduct in-service workshops at your school.
Each consultant is highly qualified and in tune with the needs of classroom teachers.

Call Rauna Twaddle for complete details at **1-800-852-1234**

YOU CAN HELP!

The National Center for Missing & Exploited Children has provided the Teaching & Learning Company with photographs of children they are attempting to locate. You CAN HELP! Please post a copy of this page in your faculty lounge. Thank you! ANYONE WITH INFORMATION SHOULD CONTACT the National Center for Missing & Exploited Children at **1-800-843-5678**.

Heather Ann Carr

Missing From: Salem, OR
Age Disappeared: 3 Yr

Missing: 08/01/92	**Weight:** 70 lbs
Age Now: 8 Yr	**Height:** 3'1"
Birth: 10/02/88	**Hair:** Light Brown
Sex: F	**Eyes:** Hazel
Race: White	

Child's eye color changes from blue to hazel/green. Her hair turns blonde during the summer.

Aaron David Carr

Missing From: Salem, OR
Age Disappeared: 2 Yr

Missing: 08/01/92	**Weight:** 60 lbs
Age Now: 7 Yr	**Height:** 2'6"
Birth: 10/20/89	**Hair:** Blonde
Sex: M	**Eyes:** Hazel
Race: White	

Child's eye color changes from blue to hazel/green.

Margaret Isabel L. Sandige

Missing From: Phoenix, AZ
Age Disappeared: 6 Yr

Missing: 10/22/94	**Weight:** 46 lbs
Age Now: 8 Yr	**Height:** 3'7"
Birth: 09/16/88	**Hair:** Brown
Sex: F	**Eyes:** Blue
Race: White Hisp	

Child speaks Spanish and English.

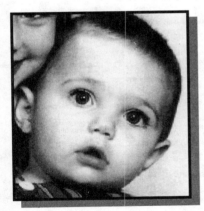

William Bruno Leon Sandige

Missing From: Phoenix, AZ
Age Disappeared: 12 Mo

Missing: 10/22/94	**Weight:** 30 lbs
Age Now: 3 Yr	**Height:** 2'6"
Birth: 10/05/93	**Hair:** Brown
Sex: M	**Eyes:** Blue
Race: White Hisp	

Cynthia Michelle Malone

Missing From: Pauls Valley, OK
Age Disappeared: 3 Yr

Missing: 05/17/95	**Weight:** 45 lbs
Age Now: 5 Yr	**Height:** 3'6"
Birth: 06/13/91	**Hair:** Blonde
Sex: F	**Eyes:** Blue
Race: White	

Child's race is also American Indian.

Shannon Nicole Malone

Missing From: Pauls Valley, OK
Age Disappeared: 2 Yr

Missing: 05/17/95	**Weight:** 30 lbs
Age Now: 3 Yr	**Height:** 2'4"
Birth: 04/13/93	**Hair:** Blonde
Sex: F	**Eyes:** Blue
Race: White	

Child's race is also American Indian.

YOU CAN HELP! 1-800-843-5678

ALABAMA

Athens–Bee Bright School Supply
Birmingham–Burrow School Supply
Birmingham–Sweetreats/DBA The Teacher's Pet
Camden–LMP School Supply
Decatur–The Learning Tree
Dothan–Tri-Angle School Supply
Gadsden–Off Campus, Inc.
Hoover–Parent Teacher Store (Southern School Supply)
Huntsville–Off Campus College Book Store
Huntsville–Schoolcraft
Jasper–The Class Room Connection
Mobile–Pencil Co.
Mobile–Summer Bookstore/DBA Anders Bookstore
Muscle Shoals–School Days
Northport–Learning Experiences
Opelika–The Apple Tree
Semmes–Educator's Resource
Tuscaloosa–Walker School Supply

ALASKA

Anchorage–Schoolhouse Express
Fairbanks–Schoolhouse Express
Juneau–The Learning Store
Wasilla–One Step Beyond

ARIZONA

Flagstaff–Northern Arizona University Bookstore
Mesa–Storybooks
Mesa–Teach & Play Smart #105
Mesa–Teaching Tools
Phoenix–School Stuff Educational Supply
Phoenix–Teach & Play Smart #104
Phoenix–Teaching Tools (Two locations)
Tempe–Teaching Tools
Tucson–Jonathan's Educational Resources (Two locations)
Tucson–Teacher Parent Connection, Inc.
Tucson–Teaching Tools

ARKANSAS

Batesville–The Schoolmarm
Fayetteville–The Education Station
Jonesboro–Landmark Books
Little Rock–Mardel, Inc.
North Little Rock–Mardel, Inc.
Rogers–Moser Corporation
Sherwood–A-Plus Teaching Supplies

CALIFORNIA

Arcadia–Alpha Plus Ed'l. & Office Supply Inc.
Bakersfield–GW School Supply
Bakersfield–The Learning Stop
Buena Park–Teachers' Supplies
Camarillo–Bright Ideas for Learning
Capitola–Kaleidoscope
Chico–The Creative Apple
Chula Vista–Educational Supplies Plus
Citrus Heights–The Report Card
Colton–Little Red Schoolhouse
Compton–Compton Teacher Connection
Concord–Warren's Educational Supplies
Costa Mesa–ESP/Teacher's Pet
Costa Mesa–The Sycamore Tree
Covina–Warren's Educational Supplies
Culver City–Social Studies School Service
Downey–Teacher's Apple
Encinitas–ESP/Teacher's Pet
Escondido–ESP/Teacher's Pet
El Cajon–ESP/Teacher's Pet
Encino–Friends of La Teacher Center
Eureka–Moon's Play N Learn
Fair Oaks–Toys That Teach
Foster City–Cayton Resources
Foster City–Tout About Toys
Fremont–Teachers' Helper
Fresno–Geography Challenge
Fresno–GW School Supply
Fullerton–C.M. School Supply
Garden Grove–U.S. Toy Company
Gilroy–Young Learning Company
Glendale–Young Scholar
Goleta–Bennett's Educational Materials
Laguna Hills–ESP/Teacher's Pet
Laguna Niguel–Teacher Supplies of Long Bch.
Lancaster–Parent-Teacher Aids
Long Beach–Teacher Supplies of Long Beach
Los Altos–Adventure Toys & Teacher's Supplies
Los Angeles–Teacher Center
Modesto–Basics Plus
Modesto–The Teacher's Aid
Montclair–Little Red Schoolhouse
Napa–Learning Faire
Northridge–Education Station
Orange–ESP/Teacher's Pet
Pasadena–Angels School Supply
Pleasant Hill–The Golden Apple
Pleasanton–The Golden Apple
Pomona–C.M. School Supply
Poway–Wiz Kid
Redding–School Tools
Reseda–Lewis for Books
Riverside–CM School Supply
Riverside–Little Red Schoolhouse
Rosemead–Warren's Educational Supplies
Rowland Hgts.–Yale Teacher Supplies
Sacramento–GW School Supply
Sacramento–The Report Card
Salinas–Educational Stuff, Inc.
San Diego–ESP/Teacher's Pet
San Diego–Wiz Kid
San Jose–Learning Rainbow
San Jose–Teachers' Helper (Two locations)
San Rafael–Marin Teacher's Store
San Ramon–The Golden Apple
Santa Maria–Rainbow Connection
Saugus–Parent Teacher Aids
Soquel–QTL Corporation–West Coast
Suisun City–The Chalkboard
Temecula–A+ Teaching Materials
Thousand Oaks–New Horizons
Upland–CM School Supply Company
Van Nuys–Educative Toys & Supplies
Ventura–Bennett's Educational Materials
Victorville–Club Ed
Visalia–Schoolworks
Whittier–Farrell's Educational Center
Winnetka–A–1 Educational Supplies & Toys
Yuba City–School House

COLORADO

Arvada–Teacher's Helper
Aurora–Banks School Supply
Aurora–Teacher's Helper
Boulder–Flearn, Inc.
Colorado Springs–Clever Camel
Colorado Springs–School Crossing
Colorado Springs–Teacher's Pet/Banks School Supply
Denver–Bookies
Denver–Colborn's
Denver–Tattered Cover Book Store
Englewood–U.S. Toy Company
Fort Collins–Stephenson School Supply
Greeley–Learning Place
Grand Junction–Better Books and Tchng. Aids
Lakewood–Great Books &Gifts
Littleton–Teacher's Helper

CONNECTICUT

Colchester–S & S Arts and Crafts Worldwide
Danbury–Teacher-Parent Store
Hartford–hpk Educational Resource Center
Manchester–Hammett's Learning World
Milford–The School Bag
Waterbury–Good Ideas

DELAWARE

Dover–Capitol Office Products
Milford–Teacher's Depot
Millsboro–The Classroom Corner
Newark–The Learning Station
Wilmington–The Frog Shoppe, Inc.

DISTRICT OF COLUMBIA

Washington, D.C.–Crown Educational Supply

FLORIDA

Apopka–Tools for Teaching
Apopka–U.S. Toy Company
Auburndale–Early Learning School Supply
Boynton Beach–Kradle to Kindergarten Bookhouse
Brandon–Teacher's Helper, Inc.
Cape Coral–School Stuff
Clearwater–J.L. Hammett Co.
Davie–Ace Educational Supplies
DeLand–The Apple Tree
Dunedin–The Learning Scene
Eustis–The Teacher's Apple
Fort Myers–School Stuff
Gainesville–The Learning Path
Jacksonville–All Florida School Supply
Jacksonville–The Polished Apple
Holly Hill–The Apple Tree
Lakeland–Schoolhouse, Inc.
Lake Mary–Schoolhouse Books and Gifts
Land O Lakes–The Gingham Goose School Supply
Leesburg–Wise Owl
Longwood–Miller's School Supply
Melbourne–The Education Station
Miami–Get Smart
Miami–Real Way School Supply
Milton–School Tools
Naples–The Wise Old Owl
North Lauderdale–Ace Educational Supplies
Ocala–The Learning Wheel
Orlando–Central Florida School Supply
Orlando–Miller's School Supply
Panama City–Learning Shoppe Ed. Supplies
Pensacola–J.L. Hammett Co.
Plantation–Ace Educational Supplies
Plantation–Teach & Play Smart #102
Port Charlotte–The Schoolbox
Port Richey–The Learning Station
Rockledge–The Education Station
Sebring–Happy Owl
St. Augustine–Teacher's Corner, Inc.
St. Petersburg–Timothy's Toys
Stuart–Teacher's Pet & More
Tallahassee–Big Bend Parent-Teacher Store
Tallahassee–Big Bend School Supply
Tampa–Big Bend Parent-Teacher Store
Tampa–An Educational Rainbow
Titusville–Instruction Junction
Vero Beach–Children's Learning Center
West Palm Beach–Stop, Look & Learn

GEORGIA

Alpharetta–The School Box, Inc.
Athens–The Apple Tree
Atlanta–ABC Parent/Teacher Learning Center
Atlanta–J.L. Hammett Co.
Atlanta–Key's Learning World
Augusta–School Days Supply Co. (Two locations)
Austell–The School Box, Inc.
Brunswick–Adam's Apple
Buford–Classroom Depot
Columbus–The School House
Conyers–Parent Teacher & Office Supply
Dalton–A-2-Z School Supplies
Duluth–ABC School Supply
Duluth–The School Box, Inc.
East Cobb–The School Box
Evans–Bright Ideas School Supply Company
Fayetteville–The Fayette Book Shop
Gainesville–The Apple Core, Inc.
Gwinnett–The School Box
Hinesville–School Days
Kennesaw–The School Box, Inc. (Two locations)
Lawrenceville–Gwinnet School Supply
Macon–GA School Supply
Marietta–The School Box, Inc.
Martinez–Bright Ideas School Supply Co.
Milledgeville–The Book Corner/The Lrng. Loft
Morrow–The School Box, Inc.
Newnan–Parent Teacher & Office Supply
North Point–The School Box
Peachtree City–Peachtree Education Station, Inc.
Riverdale–Key's Learning World
Rome–The School Box, Inc.
Roswell–ABC School Supply
Savannah–Barnett Educational Supply
Savannah–Keys of Learning
Savannah–The Teaching Tree
Snellville–Gwinnet School Supply
Statesboro–The Teaching Tree
Stockbridge–Key's Learning World
Thomasville–Shapes & More
Tucker–The School Box, Inc.
Valdosta–The Learning Tree
Willacoochee–Lindsey's

HAWAII

Aiea–Hands-On, Inc.
Hilo–B.I.B.L.E.
Honolulu–Child's Play
Honolulu–Film Services of Hawaii
Wailuku–3 R's Learning Company
Waipahu–Teacher Plus

IDAHO

Ammon–School Things & Other Things
Boise–Creative Choice
Boise–Kirtland's Idaho Book & School Supply
Boise–Teacher's Pet
Coeur d'Alene–Book & Game Company
Idaho Falls–Tools for Learning
Moscow–The Education Connection
Pocatello–Tools for Learning
Rexburg–Tools for Learning

ILLINOIS

Arlington Hgts.–J.L. Hammett Co.
Aurora–The Chalkboard
Aurora–M.P.I. Teacher Store #5
Belleville–The Teacher's Aid
Bloomingdale–The Learning Post
Bradley–The Learning Tree
Buffalo Grove–The Learning Post
Calumet–School Stuff, Inc.
Carthage–Toyasaurus Rex
Champaign–Mrs. B's School Tools
Chicago–The Classmate, Ltd.
Chicago–Gray's Dist., Inc./The Learning Tree
Chicago–Storehouse of Knowledge
Country Club Hills–Teacher's Storehouse of Knowledge
Crystal Lake–Office Mart
Crystal Lake–The Schoolhouse
Danville–Shick Supply & Equipment
Decatur–Mrs. B's Teacher Exchange Store
Decatur–Sattley's Inc.
Elgin–Teachers Apple
Effingham–The Class Menagerie
Evergreen Park–School Bell
Galesburg–Stepping Stone
Geneva–The Scholarship
Joliet–The Chalkboard
Kankakee–Tools for Schools
Lake Zurich–Off the Ceiling
Marion–Eastwood's Art & Teacher
Mattoon–Mrs. B's Teacher Supply
Moline–Wise Owl, Inc.
Murphysboro–Lindsey's Corner
Naperville–The Chalkboard
Naperville–The Learning Depot, Inc.
Oakbrook–J.L. Hammett Co.
Oak Park–Bright Ideas Parent/Teacher Store, Inc.
O'Fallon–Parent/Teacher Tools, Inc.
Palatine–Learning Express
Peoria–The School House
Quincy–Learning Adventures
Rockford–The 3 R's Learning Materials Ltd.
Salem–The Apple Branch
Schaumburg–Educational Aids, Inc.
Skokie–U.S. Toy Company
Springfield–The School Bag
Tinley Park–Teacher's Corner
Waukegan–The Teacher's Market, Inc.
West Dundee–Let's Learn
Westmont–Let's Learn

INDIANA

Anderson–The Knowledge Shoppe
Bloomington–Learning Treasures
Clarksville–Kentucky School Services
Evansville–Classroom Paraphernalia
Evansville–The Teacher's Aid, Inc.
Fort Wayne–The Learning House
Fort Wayne–United Art & Education
Hammond–School Stuff, Inc.
Hobart–Sharp School Services, Inc.
Indianapolis–Education Galore
Indianapolis–Learning Shop
Indianapolis–Parent/Teacher Ed. World (Three locations)
Indianapolis–Seeds for Knowledge (Two locations)
Indianapolis–United Art & Education
Jasper–The Teacher's Aid, Inc.
Kokomo–Teacher's Delight
Lafayette–Teacher's Delight
Logansport–The Polished Apple
Merrillville–School Stuff, Inc.
Michigan City–School Stuff, Inc.
Plainfield–The Learning Depot
South Bend–Creative Teaching, Inc.
Terre Haute–Parent Teacher Education World
Valparaiso–Koala T. Learning

IOWA

Bettendorf–Wise Owl, Inc.
Burlington–Typewriter Shop
Cedar Falls–School Specialty
Council Bluffs–Learning Explorations, Inc. D/B/A Learning Tools
Dubuque–Wise Owl, Inc.
Fort Madison–The Chalkboard
Marion–Wise Owl, Inc.
Sioux City–Kvam's
West Des Moines–The Learning Post

KANSAS

Lawrence–School Specialties
Leawood–U.S. Toy Company
Manhattan–The Learning Factory
Overland Park–Hammett's Teaching Tools
Overland Park–The Supply Closet (Two locations)
Pittsburg–Bowlus School Supply
Salina–School Specialty Supply
Salina–Superior School & Office
Wichita–Superior School Supplies

KENTUCKY

Bowling Green–Southern School Supply
Covington–John R. Green Company
Danville–The School Box, Inc.
Elizabethtown–Kentucky School Service
Florence–Central School Supply, Inc.
Henderson–Sixteenth Section
Lexington–Educator's Delight
Lexington–Parent Teacher Store (Southern School Supply)
London–The Supply Center, Inc.
Louisville–Central School Supply, Inc.
Louisville–Kentucky School Service (Two locations)
Louisville–Parent Teacher Store (Two locations)
Maysville–The Learning Corner
Murray–Murray State University Bookstore
Owensboro–The Teacher's Aid
Winchester–The Elephant's Trunk

LOUISIANA

Abbeville–Teacher's Choice
Alexandria–School Aids
Arabi–Alpha Office & Educational Inc.
Baker–Creative Educational Supplies
Baton Rouge–School Aids (Two locations)
Breaux Bridge–Blanchard's Ed. Supply
Deridder–Author's Alley
Gretna–Educator, Inc.
Harahan–Educator, Inc.
Kenner–Educator, Inc.
Lafayette–J & R Educational
Metairie–Educator, Inc.
Monroe–The Teacher's Mart
Natchitoches–Campus Corner
New Iberia–Apple Core
Ruston–Smith's Teacher Supply
Shreveport–Paula's Educational Supplies
Slidell–Education Station
Thibodaux–Lee's Educational Center, Inc.
Ville Platte–Bell Office Supply Inc.

MAINE

Auburn–Rhyme & Reason
Augusta–ABACUS–The Learning Store
Augusta–The Painted Horse
Bangor–ABACUS–The Learning Store
Caribous–Boise Cascade Office Products
South Portland–The Painted Horse

MARYLAND

Annapolis–learn'ing how
Baltimore–J.L. Hammett Co.
Baltimore–learn'ing how
Columbia–learn'ing how
Fallston–Professor Bear's Country
Frederick–Frederick Office Supply
Frederick–learn'ing how
Gaithersburg–Crown Ed. & Teaching Aids
Gambrills–A+ Education Etc.
Mitchellville–Educational, Etc.
Oakland–Mark IV Office Supply
Rockville–ABC's & 123's
Salisburg–Educational Supplies, Inc.
Towson–learn'ing how

MASSACHUSETTS

Agawam–School Specialty
Braintree–J.L. Hammett Co.
Cambridge–Sandy and Son Ed. Supplies
Chicopee–Time to Teach
Fitchburg–Teacher's Helper
Holyoke–J.L. Hammett Co.
Lawrence–The Teacher's Pet, Inc.
Marlborough–J.L. Hammett Co.
Natick–Edu-Mart
Natick–J.L. Hammett Co.
N. Attleboro–Hammett's Learning World
North Dartmouth–Up with Learning
Norwell–A Wing & A Prayer
Norwood–The Learning Well
Plainville–The Learning Link
Plymouth–A Wing & A Prayer
Seekonk–The Paper Scene
Seekonk–Up with Learning
Shrewsbury–Spags Supply
Waltham–The Holt Company
Worcester–The Teachers Store

MICHIGAN

Alanson–The School Store
Battle Creek–The Learning Link of Battle Creek
Bay City–Education Express
Brighton–Parent Teacher Tech Center
Grand Rapids–Debby & Company
Grand Rapids–Grow & Learn
Grand Rapids–M.P.I. Teacher Store #3
Kalamazoo–Teacher's Center
Lansing–M.P.I. Teacher Store #4
Lansing–Teaching Connection
Livonia–M.P.I. Teacher Store #1
Midland–School Days
Monroe–Schoolbox Supplies
Muskegon–Hage's Christian Supplies
Novi–The Learning Tree
Saginaw–Educator's Warehouse, Inc.
St. Clair Shores–Knowledge Nook
St. Joseph–Creative Teaching, St. Joe
St. Paul–Hands On Education
St. Paul–St. Paul Book & Stationery
Shelby Twp.–The Learning Tree
Southgate–Erasers & Crayons
Sterling Heights–The Learning Tree
Sterling Heights–M.P.I. Teacher Store #2
Traverse City–Country Schoolhouse
Waterford–The Learning Tree
Warren–1, 2, 3 Outlet

MINNESOTA

Apple Valley–Hands on Education
Arden Hills–St. Paul Book & Stationery
Bloomington–Pencils & Play
Bloomington–School Stuff, Inc.
Burnsville–Classroom Connections
Crystal–Classroom Connections
Duluth–Explorations Educators
Duluth–St. Paul Book & Stationery
Eden Prairie–St. Paul Book & Stationery
Edina–St. Paul Book & Stationery
Mankato–St. Paul Book & Stationery
Maplewood–St. Paul Book & Stationery
Minnetonka–St. Paul Book & Stationery
Norwest–St. Paul Book & Stationery
Oakdale–Classroom Connections
St. Cloud–The Bookworm
St. Paul–St. Paul Book & Stationery
South St. Paul–Creative Educational Materials

MISSISSIPPI

Columbus–School Stuff
Greenville–Learning Links
Gulfport–Europe's Finest Teacher Corner
Gulfport–School & Carnival Supply
Hattiesburg–Curiosity Shoppe
Ocean Springs–S & S Supply Co.
Ridgeland–Education Mart
Ridgeland–School Aids, Inc.

MISSOURI

Ballwin–Bradburn Parent Teacher Store
Ballwin–Classic Classrooms
Cape Girardeau–3R's Plus Supplies
Columbia–Ann's Teacher Store & More
Creve Coeur–Bradburn Parent Teacher Store
Ellisville–Bradburn Parent Teacher Store
Grandview–U.S. Toy Co., Inc.
Independence–The Teacher's Store
Jefferson City–A+ Educational Materials
Joplin–J.R. Learning
Kansas City–KC Kids Teacher Supply
Kansas City–Learning Exchange
Kirkwood–The Learning Curve
Lebanon–Apple Days Educ. Supply
Lee's Summit–The Supply Closet
O'Fallon–Best Office & School Supply
St. Charles–Book Mark
St. Joseph–Pigtails 'N' Inkwells
St. Louis–Bradburn School Supply, Inc.
St. Louis–Classroom Connections
St. Louis–J.L. Hammett Co.
Sikeston–Craftmasters
Springfield–Goldminds
Springfield–IPA Educational Supply
Springfield–Southwest Missouri State University Bookstore
Warrenton–Schoolhouse Books

MONTANA

Billings–Colborn's
Bozeman–The Learning Source
Butte–Magic Castle
Kalispell–Teacher's Pet
Kalispell–The Village Book Shop
Missoula–Great Northern Book Company
Missoula–The Learning Tree

NEBRASKA

Alliance–Iris's Special Things
Gering–Teacher's Corner
Grand Island–Stephenson School

products are available at . . .

Teaching & Learning Company

Supply
Lincoln–Stephenson School School Supply (Two locations)
Lincoln–The Learning Station
Omaha–The Learning Station
Omaha–Playtime Equipment
Omaha–Stephenson School Supply (Two locations)

NEVADA
Henderson–Learning Is Fun
Las Vegas–Learning Is Fun (Two locations)
Reno–Parent Teacher Aids
Sparks–Apple School Supply

NEW HAMPSHIRE
Hooksett–Teach and Learn Shop
Keene–Learn & Play
Laconia–Motivate & Educate
North Conway–Toy Chest
West Lebanon–Help-U-Teach

NEW JERSEY
Cherry Hill–Teacher Store (Becker & Bro., Inc.)
Colts Neck–It's Elementary
Denville–Keys to Learning
Freehold–Hammett's Learning World
Egg Harbor Township–Learning Can Be Fun
Hackensack–Teacher Store (Becker & Bro., Inc.)
Lawrenceville–Interstate Media Co.
Mercerville–Learning Partners
Middletown–A+ Educational Resources
Middletown–Wendy Drug, Inc.
Mitchellville–Educational, Etc.
Morristown–The Teaching Room
Pennsauken–Roberts Brothers, Inc.
Phillipsburg–J.L. Hammett Co.
Pitman–Learning Can Be Fun
Pt. Pleasant Beach–Borden's Stationery
Raritan–The Teaching Room
Saddle Brook–Bosland's Learning Plus, Inc.
Sparta–The Teacher's Store & More
Tom's River–J.L. Hammett Co.
Verona–J.L. Hammett Co.
Voorhees–Hammett's Learning World
Watchung–Teacher Store (Becker & Bro., Inc.)
Woodbridge–J.L. Hammett Co.

NEW MEXICO
Albuquerque–Allied School & Office Products
Albuquerque–Colborn's
Farmington–Educate-Um
Gallup–Butler's Office Equipment & Supplies
Roswell–Dabs–Teacher Store

NEW YORK
Albany–Hammett's Learning World
Allegany–Education First
Bronx–Teacher's Stuff
Brooklyn–Barclay School Supplies
Buffalo–Paul's Teacher's Pet
Clay–J.L. Hammett Co.
Elmira–Teacher Time
Endicott–Satico's Parent Teacher Center
Farmingdale–L.L. Weans
Flushing–Carol School Supply, Inc.
Ithaca–Teaching Treasures
Kingston–Parent Teacher Store
Latham–Parent Teacher Store
Medford–Island School and Art Supply
Middletown–Hammett's Learning World
Middletown–Teacher Center
Mineola–W. Warner, Inc.
Nanuet–A+ and Educational Warehouse
New Windsor–Ariel's Child
Poughkeepsie–J.L. Hammett Co.
Poughkeepsie–Golden Apples Ed. Materials
Queens Village–Nick Breglio, Inc.
Riverhead–East End School Supply
Rochester–Paul's Teacher's Pet
Rochester–Teacher's World
Rockville Center–The Creative Child
Saint Albans–Warner Educational Supplies
Saratoga Springs–Soave'faire, Inc.
Saratoga Springs–Teaching Toys and Supplies
Schenectady–Apple Source
Staten Island–Hammett's Learning World
Staten Island–The Learning Tree
Utica–ABC Express
Watertown–School Daze
White Plains–Teacher's Room

NORTH CAROLINA
Arden–Teacher's Edition
Asheville–Morgan's School Supply
Asheville–Teacher's Edition
Belmont–School Specialties
Charlotte–Goldi Adventures in Learning
Charlotte–J.L. Hammett Co. (Two locations)
Charlotte–Parent Teacher Store (Southern School Supply)
Dunn–Knowledge Unlimited
Durham–Not Just Paper
Fayetteville–School Tools
Fayetteville–Parker School & Office Supply
Fayetteville–School Zone . . . (Paper, Pens, Etc.)
Goldsboro–The Learning Center, Inc.
Greensboto–Edu-Play
Greensboto–Kids Lore
Greenville–Bender-Burkot School Supply
Havelock–Cover to Cover Bookstore
Hickory–Creative Learning
Jacksonville–Autry Parent/Teacher & Office Supply Co.
Jacksonville–The Polished Apple
Kannapolis–The Designer Desk
Kernersville–I.E.S.S., Inc.
Morehead City–Teacher's Pet
Newton–Education Station
Pittsburgh–Holcomb's
Raleigh–The Creative Teacher
Raleigh–J.L. Hammett Co.
Raleigh–Stones School Supply
Raleigh–The Teach Me Store
Rocky Mount–The Book Shoppe
Salisbury–Creative Teaching Aids
Shelby–Education Station
Whiteville–Teachers R Special & Parents, Too
Wilmington–Teacher's Aid
York–Education Station

NORTH DAKOTA
Minot–The Teacher's Aid
Mandan–The Learning Fair, Inc.

OHIO
Akron–Creative Curriculum
Bellefontaine–Education Station
Bluffton–Edu-Caterers
Bridgeville–Holcomb's
Canton–Curriculum Concepts
Canton–Wise Owl
Cincinnati–Central School Supply (Three locations)
Cleveland–Holcomb's
Columbus–Holcomb's (Two locations)
Columbus–Teacher's Helper East
Cuyahoga Falls–Holcomb's
Dayton–F & S Enterprises
Dayton–Holcomb's
Delaware–Fundamentals
Holland–Holcomb's
Lima–Edu-Caterers
Lima–Educational Providers
Marion–ABC Educational Supply
Mayfield Heights–Holcomb's
Medina–Ahead of the Class
Monroesville–Holcomb's
New Philadelphia–Bright Ideas
Niles–Teaching Things, Inc.
North Olmstead–Holcomb's
Painesville–Teacher's Corner
Reynoldsburg–Teacher's Helper East
St. Mary's–Edu-Caterers
Toledo–ABC Center
Upper Arlington–Inquiring Minds
Westerville–Teacher's Helper East
Youngstown–Holcomb's
Youngstown–The Supplyroom, Inc.

OKLAHOMA
Apache–Sexton & Sexton School Supply
Edmond–Mardel, Inc.
Hulbert–McGowan School Supply & Service
Midwest City–Mardel, Inc.
Muskogee–The Learning Ladder
Norman–Copelin's Office Center
Norman–Mardel, Inc.
Oklahoma City–Classroom Connections (Two locations)
Oklahoma City–Mardel, Inc. (Three locations)
Tulsa–The Apple Tree
Tulsa–Friends of Day Care
Tulsa–The Learning Shop
Tulsa–Mardel, Inc. (Two locations)
Weatherford–Hooked on Books

OREGON
Ashland–The Tree House
Beaverton–Learning Palace
Eugene–Learning Palace
Eugene–School Daze
Gresham–Learning Palace
LaGrande–Eastern Oregon State College Bookstore
Medford–Clas E. Professor
Portland–Learning Palace
Salem–School Daze
Tigard–School Daze

PENNSYLVANIA
Camp Hill–The Learning Source
Churchville–Aristotle's Notebook
Cleona–The Resource Island
Cranberry Township–School Days Supply Shop
DuBois–Rosie's Book Shop
Erie–Inside the Jelly Jar
Erie–Little Professor Book Center
Erie–Teaching Touches
Feasterville–Aristotle's Notebook
Grove City–School Days Supply Shop
Harrisburg–Edu-Care Services, Inc.
Harrisburg–The Learning Source
Harrisburg–QTL Corporation–East Coast
Lancaster–Education Station
Lancaster–The Learning Store
Lock Haven–The Bus Stops Here
McMurray–The Chalkboard
Meadville–Teaching Touches
New Castle–Head of the Class
North Wales–U.S. Toy Company
Philadelphia–Charles J. Becker & Bro. Inc.
Philadelphia–Teacher Store (Becker & Bro., Inc.)
Pittsburgh–Holcomb's
Reading–Educational & Fun Ltd.
Rochester–Radella's School World
Roslyn–Paine Learning Aids Center
Sayre–Jane's Book Nook
Scottdale–Mark IV Office Supply
Seneca–One Stop Education Shop
Shippensburg–University Store
Springfield–Teacher Store (Becker & Bro., Inc.)
State College–Kurtz Korner
Uniontown–Little Printing Company
Waynesburg–Mark IV Office Supply
West Chester–School House Supplies, Inc. (Two locations)
York–Education Station

RHODE ISLAND
Cranston–Up with Learning
Johnston–The Teacher's Room

SOUTH CAROLINA
Aiken–Creative Program Planners
Anderson–Anderson Education Center
Barnwell–The Bookworm
Beaufort–Alphabet Soup Educational Supply
Charleston–J.L. Hammett Co.
Charleston–The Learning Center
Columbia–Educational Wonderland (Two locations)
Goose Creek–Educational Wonderland
Goose Creek–The Learning Center
Greenville–J.L. Hammett Co.
Greenwood–McCaslan's Book Store
Myrtle Beach–Teacher's Touch, Inc.
Newberry–Armfield's, Inc.
Orangeburg–Palmetto Office Supply
Seneca–Learning Safari
Spartanburg–Evans Office Supply, Inc.
Taylors–Teacher's Choice

SOUTH DAKOTA
Rapid City–Book & Company
Rapid City–Parent Teacher Outlet
Sioux Falls–Teaching Treasures
Sioux Falls–Teacher's Helper

TENNESSEE
Bartlett–Learning House
Chattanooga–P & S School & Office Supply
Clinton–Educator's Exchange (Two locations)
Dresden–A to Z 123
Dyersburg–The Learning House
Germantown–Knowledge Tree
Goodlettsville–Parent Teacher Store (Southern School Supply)
Jackson–The Learning House
Knoxville–P & S School & Office Supply
Germantown–Knowledge
Manchester–A+ School & Office Supply
Memphis–Learning House
Nashville–Parent Teacher Store (Southern School Supply)
Nashville–School Age Notes
Soddy Daisy–Tool 4 School & Office
Tullahoma–Teacher Express
Union City–The Learning House

TEXAS
Abilene–Abilene Educational Supply
Amarillo–Cashway-Plains Teaching Supply
Arlington–Classroom Connections
Arlington–Education, Inc.
Arlington–Teach & Play Smart #106
Austin–Aus-Tex Education Supply
Austin–Dick Office Supply
Austin–Good Books
Beaumont–Manning's School Supply
Brenham–T O P S
Brownsville–Jones & Cook Stationers
Brownwood–Brownwood Teaching Aids
Bryan–T O P S
Carrollton–Classroom Connections
Carrollton–U.S. Toy Company
Cleveland–The Ark
Conroe–The Schoolhouse Store
Corpus Christi–Class Success Ed. Supply (Two locations)
Corpus Christi–Corpus Christi Educational
Dallas–A Teacher's Aide
Dallas–Teach & Play Smart #101
Denton–Teacher's World
Duncanville–Ben Franklin
Edinburg–Gateway Printing & Office Supply, Inc.
El Paso–Springers
Fort Worth–Education, Inc.
Fort Worth–Teach & Play Smart #103
Grand Prairie–Teaching Tools
Greenville–Apples for the Teacher
Harker Heights–Educational Outfitters
Harlingen–Jones & Cook Stationers
Houston–Basic Office & School Supply
Houston–Coastal Office & Teacher Supply
Houston–Crystal Children & Teacher Supply
Houston–Southwest Teacher Supply (Three locations)
Houston–Star Office Supply
Humble–The Schoolhouse Store
Huntsville–The Schoolhouse Store
Hurst–Teacher's Tools
Irving–A+ Teach R
Lake Jackson–Texas Educational Resources
Laredo–Educator's Emporium
Laredo–Imagine Parent Teacher Education Ctr.
Longview–East Texas Educational Supplies
Longview–Jordan's Knowledge Nook
Lubbock–Bailey's Bookstore
Lubbock–Creative Schoolhouse, Inc.
McAllen–Dick Office Supply
McAllen–Jones & Cook Stationers
McAllen–O'Neall Specialty Company, Inc.
McAllen–Rio Grande Book Company
Mesquite–The Teacher's Store
Midland–Creative Schoolhouse, Inc.
Mount Vernon–Northeast Texas Publishing
Nacogdoches–Terrific Teacher's Treasures, Inc.
Nederland–Manning's School Supply
Odessa–Teachers' Market
Palestine–Education Unlimited
Pharr–O'Neall Specialty Company, Inc.
Plano–Classroom Connections
Plano–Diamond School Supply
Plano–Teach & Play Smart #107
Plainview–The Teacher Store
Richardson–Teaching, Etc.
Rosenberg–Texas Educational Resources
Round Rock–Good Books
San Angelo–Angelo School & Teacher Supply
San Angelo–Tools for School
San Antonio–A Brighter Child
San Antonio–Learning Zone/KIMCO Educational Products
San Antonio–Schoolocker Teacher Supply
San Juan–The Classic Twist
Spring–The Schoolhouse Store
Stephenville–The Apple Tree
Temple–The Teacher's Store
Texarkana–Learning Center
Tyler–Get Copy Printing & Educational Products
Victoria–Victoria Teaching/Office Supply
Waco–The Learning Center
Waxahachie–Teacher's Touch
Weslaco–Jones & Cook Stationers
Wichita Falls–Mardel, Inc.
Wichita Falls–The Red Apple

UTAH
Bountiful–Learning Systems
Cedar City–Mountain West Office Supply
Layton–Utah Idaho Supply/Map World
Murray–Utah Idaho Supply/Map World
Ogden–Utah Idaho Supply/Map World
Orem–Discovery Educational
Provo–Little Dickens
Salt Lake City–The Alphabet Station
Salt Lake City–Utah Idaho Supply/Map World

VERMONT
Essex Junction–M.D.P School Supply

VIRGINIA
Bristol–Kentucky School Service
Centerville–Crown Educational Supply
Charlottesville–Teacher's Edition
Chesapeake–Parent-Teacher Supply Co.
Chesapeake–TAPS, Teachers & Parents Store, Inc.
Chesapeake–Teacher's Edition
Danville–The Learning Source
Fairfax–K.T.'s Inc.
Fredericksburg–Teacher's Edition #1
Glen Allen–J.L.Hammett Co.
Hampton–TAPS, Teachers & Parents Store, Inc.
Kenbridge–Kenbridge Office & School Supply
Lynchburg–Little Dickens
Manassas–Teacher's Edition #2
Martinsville–Teacher's Pet
Newport News–The Teacher's Store
Norfolk–J.L. Hammett Co.
Oakton–J.L. Hammett Co.
Richmond–Teach N' Things
Roanoke–Kentucky School Service
Roanoke–The Learning Source
Springfield–J.L. Hammett Co.
Stafford–The Scholar Ship
Staunton–B & B Educational Supplies
Tabb–Parent-Teacher Supply Co.
Virginia Beach–TAPS, Teachers & Parents Store, Inc. (Two locations)
Winchester–Learning Locker, Inc.
Woodbridge–School & Office Annex

WASHINGTON
Aberdeen–The Thought Shop
Edmonds–Basic Educational Books
Ellensburg–Creative Concepts
Ellensburg–University Store
Everett–The Creative Teacher
Kent–Children's Bookshop
Olympia–School Daze
Seattle–Pacific Science Center
Seattle–Tickle Tune Typhoon
Selah–The Teacher's Desk
Spokane–Whiz Kids (Two locations)
Spokane–Children's Corner Bookshop
Vancouver–Learning Palace
Washougal–Hewitt Research Foundation

WEST VIRGINIA
Clarksburg–The James & Law Company
Fairmont–Educational Resource Center
Huntington–Latta's School Supplies
Parkersburg–EEI/Teacher/Parent Store
South Charleston–Parent Teacher Store (Southern School Supply)
South Charleston–School Days
Wheeling–Imperial Display

WISCONSIN
Appleton–Learning Shop
Appleton–School Specialty
Ashland–The Treehouse
Brookfield–Teacher's Pet, Inc.
Brown Port–Teacher's Pet, Inc.
Eau Claire–Pencils & Play, Ltd.
Green Bay–The School House
Janesville–Stories & Stuff
Janesville–Toad'ly Kids
Kenosha–The Red Bell
Madison–Highsmith Education Station
Madison–Learning Shop (Two locations)
Milwaukee–U R Special
Onalaska–Learning Shop
Racine–The Red Bell
Richland–Teacher's Stuff
Schofield–Play 'N Learn
Shorewood–Teacher's Pet, Inc.
Stevens Point–Play 'N Learn
Wausau–Toad'ly Kids
Wauwatosa–Teacher's Pet, Inc.
West Allis–Teacher's Pet, Inc.

CANADA
Altona, Manitoba–D.W. Friesen and Sons Ltd.
Arnprior, Ontario–Arnprior Book Shop
Barrie, Ontario–ECE Supply
Barrie, Ontario–Moyer's
Brampton, Ontario–Moyer's
Burnaby, BC–Moyer's
Calgary, Alberta–Brennan Educ. Supply Ltd.
Calgary, Alberta–Kids Are Worth It!
Calgary, Alberta–Moyer's (Two locations)
Calgary, Alberta–Treehouse Books
Cote St. Luc, Quebec–Moyer's
Dartmouth, Novia Scotia –Moyer's
Dieppe, New Brunswick–Moyer's
Edmonton, Alberta–Kids Are Worth It!
Edmonton, Alberta–Moyer's (Three locations)
Edmonton, Alberta–Western Educ. Activities
Fort St. John, BC–Playful Learning
Fredericton, New Brunswick–Moyer's
Guelph, Ontario–Kids Are Worth It!
Halifax, Nova Scotia–Kids Are Worth It!
Halifax, Nova Scotia–Moyer's
Hamilton, Ontario–Moyer's (Two locations)
Kelowna, BC–Learner's World
Kitchener, Ontario–Moyer's
Kitchener, Ontario–Scholar's Choice
Langley, BC–Moyer's
Lethbridge, Alberta–Moyer's
London, Ontario–Moyer's (Two locations)
London East, Ontario–Scholar's Choice
London West, Ontario–Scholar's Choice
Markham, Ontario–Scholar's Choice
Mississauga, Ontario–Kids Are Worth It!
Mississauga, Ontario–Moyer's
Mississauga, Ontario–Scholar's Choice
Montreal, Quebec–Moyer's
Nanaimo, BC–Education Station (Two locations)
Nanaimo, BC–Kool & Child
Newmarket, Ontario–Moyer's
New Westminster, BC–Moyer's
Oakville, Ontario–Kids Are Worth It!
Ottawa, Ontario–Moyer's (Two locations)
Pickering, Ontario–Kids Are Worth It!
Pointe Claire, Quebec–Moyer's
Port Coquitlam, BC–Moyer's
Regina, Saskatchewan–Moyer's
Rexdale, Ontario–Moyer's
Richmond, BC–Moyer's
Richmond Hill, Ontario–Kids Are Worth It!
St. Catharines, Ontario–Moyer's
Saskatoon, Saskatchewan–Saskatoon Book Store, Inc.
Scarborough, Ontario–Moyer's (Two locations)
Sudbury, Ontario–Scholar's Choice
Sudbury, Ontario–The Classroom
Toronto, Ontario–Kids Are Worth It!
Vancouver, BC–Collins Educational
Vernon, BC–Vernon Teach & Learn
Waterloo, Ontario–Moyer's
West Vancouver, BC–Kids Are Worth It!
Whitby, Ontario–Teach EEZ
Williams Lake, BC–Playful Learning
Willowdale, Ontario–Moyer's (Three locations)
Windsor, Ontario–Catch a Rainbow, Inc.
Windsor, Ontario–Scholar's Choice
Winnipeg, Manitoba–Kids Are Worth It!
Winnipeg, Manitoba–Moyer's (Two locations)

FOREIGN
Buenos Aires–Nora Urban (LOOK)
London, England–Teaching Trends
Flatts, Flbx., Bermuda–Al-Mil Enterprises
Barrigada, Guam–Rainbow's End
Singapore–Integrative Learning Resources
Seneca–The Learning Safari

Save on shipping and handling!

(Visit the school supply store nearest you!)
This list effective 10/14/96.

A subscription to *Holidays & Seasonal Celebrations* is a *great* gift idea!

For yourself or for a friend!

What an exceptional magazine!
K. Frame, 3rd grade teacher
Michigan

Fill in the information below, and we'll do the rest. We'll even send your friend a special card notifying them of your gift! Call us or return this form with your check or credit card information before February 25, 1997* so you or your friend will receive the April/May/June/July issue as the first of four, big 80-page issues! All for only $17.95 ($23.95 foreign). Thank you from the Teaching & Learning Company!

* If received after February 25, 1997, the subscription will begin with the August/September/October issue as the first of four issues.

Bill To:	Ship To:
Name _____	Name _____
Address _____	Address _____
Box _____ Apt. #_____	Box _____ Apt. #_____
City _____	City _____
State _____ Zip _____ Gr. Level _____	State _____ Zip _____ Gr. Level _____
Home Phone _____	Home Phone _____
Work Phone _____	Work Phone _____

Enclosed:　　　Check　　　Money Order

Purchase Order # _____

Please charge to:　　　MasterCard　　　VISA

Acct # _____ Exp. Date _____

Signature _____

ORDER TOLL FREE
1-800-852-1234

Order from your local school supply store or mail to:

Teaching & Learning Company • Dept. MHS78 • 1204 Buchanan St., P.O. Box 10 • Carthage, IL 62321

Quantity	Item #	Title	Retail Price	Subtotal

Safety Smart

Integrate valuable lessons in safety into your regular curriculum and give your students the opportunity to make personal safety a choice and a challenge–not just a matter of luck!

Safety Smart offers students a stimulating and engaging overview of a variety of safety issues. An introductory story depicts children involved in realistic situations and authentic problems. Age-appropriate enrichment activities (discussions, dramas, puzzles, games and evaluation tools) deal with and develop the safety concerns presented in the stories.

Safety Smart–Primary has more than a dozen scenarios involving the safety issues that often face young children: fire safety, being home alone, being lost, water safety, bicycle safety, etc.

TLC10015　K-3　144 pp.　$13.95

Merchandise Total	
Shipping & Handling Costs: All orders $0-$35　Add $3.50. All orders over $35.00　Add 10%. Canada and Foreign: please remit in U.S. funds. Canada add 7% GST.	
Illinois residents, add 6.25% sales tax.	
Total for Subscription(s) (U.S.: No tax or shipping charge.)	
Total Amount Enclosed Dept. MHS78	

Teaching & Learning Company

Prices are subject to change.
Printed in the U.S.A.

Holidays & Seasonal Celebrations, Issue 8, Teaching & Learning Co. © 1997, Carthage, IL 62321